My Life With Horses

THE STORY OF JACK JUBY MBE

MASTER OF THE HEAVY HORSE

Edited by
ALISON DOWNES *and* ALAN CHILDS

Map *by* ASHLEY SAMPSON

HALSGROVE

First published in Great Britain in 2006
Reprinted 2007

British Library Cataloguing-in-Publication Data
A CIP record for this title is available from the British Library

ISBN 978 1 84114 560 0

HALSGROVE
Halsgrove House
Ryelands Industrial Estate
Bagley Road, Wellington
Somerset TA21 9PZ
Tel: 01823 653777
Fax: 01823 216796
email: sales@halsgrove.com
website: www.halsgrove.com

Printed and bound by CPI Antony Rowe Ltd., Wiltshire

EDITOR'S NOTE

The transcripts made from Jack's tapes have been used just as they are, with the exception of a few slight changes made in the interests of clarity, or to avoid repetition. Whilst every effort has been made, by the kind help of 'expert' proof-readers, to ensure that names and places are accurately given, we can only apologize for any errors caused by our lack of knowledge within the context of the time-scale covered by Jack's memory. Sadly, few people now remain who can help to verify many of the details. Where a name has not been verified, a question mark will be added. 'Norfolkisms' have quite rightly been retained, so foreigners must be prepared to 'larn the language!' Punctuation has had to be invented of course, and it is hoped this reflects Jack's style of speech. As Jack usually referred to his wife as 'Mother' rather than 'Margaret' this has been kept, other than when confusion might be caused referring to his own mother. Likewise, we have taken Jack's comments in the light-hearted spirit in which they were intended, complete with the occasional expletive, but must apologize for any offence caused, however unlikely!

DEDICATION

To my parents, Jack and Margaret, with love

And in memory of my dear sister Mavie and my dear nephew Michael

Died 17 October 2001, aged 46   Died 24 October 2002, aged 31

FOREWORD

This book has been compiled by the late Jack Juby's daughter Alison, and it is a credit to her painstaking transcribing of the tape recordings she made with her father, that she has been able to present such a detailed and readable account of country life in a period so different from today. For Jack was a true 'man of the land', born into a rural community with very little material benefits, but with a very strong affinity with the land, its demands, its challenges and its bounty. Above all, from a very early age Jack worked with horses – a bond which was forged and remained a dominant factor throughout his long life.

He soon became an outstanding handler of horses; without exception they responded to him, for he was concerned for their well-being, whatever their size or breed. This became almost a crusade with him. He rightly complained that people were required by law to receive proper training to ensure standards of safety in driving and using motor vehicles, tractors and machinery, but were simply set loose to handle their horses without any training or even supervision, and often with scant concern for the poor old horses. This worried Jack constantly, especially as there were so few agencies devoted to improving the welfare of these animals, and such little interest shown by those with power to legislate for real improvement.

The economic slumps of the 1920s and 1930s hit farming, and other economic activities on the land, particularly hard. Unemployment was rife and budgets were tight. Jack with a young family to provide for, suffered like the rest, but his resilience and attachment to the land never left him, and he struggled through.

Throughout the 1939–45 War, the tractor had become a major source of power in farming. This was of course intensified in the post-war era, and the working horse disappeared from the land. But Jack's association with his beloved 'heavies' continued with the Peacock family's stable of Percherons at Morley, Jack presenting these magnificent working horses at many major events and shows. He also served as a member of Council of the Percheron Horse Society for a number of years, and was a constant source of help and encouragement to numerous young riders and their ponies.

Jack Juby was a good man – and a realist. He recognised that horses would never again occupy a major role in the workplace or on the land, but he strove always to ensure that they did fulfil a vital function in many people's lives. This was his purpose, and those of us who knew him are thankful for the generosity and example he set.

Roderick Watt
Former President,
British Percheron Horse Society

ACKNOWLEDGEMENTS

Our very grateful thanks to everyone who has given help, and sincere apologies if any name has been omitted.

Dawn Aldous; Tony Balderstone; Gordon Bales; David Banham; Mel Barrett; John Blake; Michaela Bond (née Weir); Muriel Bond; Peggy Boyd; Tony Bradstreet; Philip Bradstreet; Jimmy Brown; Robena Brown; Edna Buckley; Mr and Mrs Frank Bush; Kenny Carter; Linda V. Chapman; Sarah Childs; Ann Chinnery; Judy Christopher; Roger Clarke; Mr and Mrs Ivan Cooke; John Coston; Lorna Downes; Oliver Downes; William Downes; *Dereham and Fakenham Times*; Mr and Mrs Kenny Eaglen; *East Anglian Daily Times*; *Eastern Daily Press*; John Ellis; Heather Evans; Mike Flood; Mr and Mrs Keith Forder; The Garner family; Joe Godderidge; Mr and Mrs William Hart; Mr and Mrs Cuthbert Hastings; *Heavy Horse World*; Frank Hewitt; John Holman; Ray Hubbard; Dick Jeeves; Joel; Alan ('Bob') Juby; Bryan Juby; Kenny Juby; Margaret Juby; Monica Mann; Christabel Manson; Kay Matson; Millennium Library, Norwich; Jill Morris (née Hewitt); Mr and Mrs Kenny Page; John Peacock; Mr and Mrs John Pennell; Mike Pollitt; Wendy Preis; Peter Prior; Christine Reeve (née Hewitt); Howard Rose; Royal Veterinary School; Philip Ryder-Davies; Ashley Sampson; Maggie Secker; Janet Skidmore; Keith Skipper; Derek Spanton; Mr and Mrs Sam Stacey; Geoff Storey; Eddy Thompson; Roderick Watts; Iris Welford; Trevor Weston; 'Roey' White (nee Juby); Diane Zeuner.

To Ashley Sampson, our sincere thanks for contributing the excellent map.

Our particular thanks to our expert proof readers/advisers for their invaluable help:
Sarah Childs; Ray Hubbard; Philip Ryder-Davies; Maggie Secker; Keith Skipper; Geoff Storey.

PHOTO CREDITS

We are extremely grateful to the following organisations and individuals who generously allowed us to use photographs or artwork:
Dawn Aldous; David Banham; Robena Brown; Linda V. Chapman; Judy Christopher; *East Anglian Daily Times*; Eastern Counties Newspapers (Archant); Associated Express Pictures; Colin Fry; Joe Godderidge; Paul Hammond; Ray Hubbard; Dick Jeeves; Alan ('Bob') Juby; Kay Matson; Dave Peacock; John Peacock; Christine Reeve (née Hewitt); Trevor Weston; 'Roey' White (née Juby); Wymondham Photographic.

CONTENTS

'The Homecoming', a watercolour based on Jack.
Reproduced by kind permission of Kay Matson

INTRODUCTION

It is often said that we live in a world bereft of real 'characters'. Although it may be difficult to define the word, most people *know* what they mean by it. It refers to men or women who make their mark, perhaps in a unique way, and for whose presence the world is a richer place. Jack Juby was essentially a character, and from his memoirs it would seem had always been so – a remarkable man by any standards. And the most remarkable gift that Jack had, was an affinity with horses. It was a relationship with horses of all types and breeds, but especially with the heavy horses, and in particular the Percherons, with which he will always be associated. It was of little surprise that when Jack returned from his one and only proper holiday to the Isle of Wight, Fen Admiral, one of his special stallions 'told' the other horses on the farm that Jack was back, and so it became a very vocal welcome home! It was no surprise either that experts, including vets, were known to consult Jack over tricky problems with their horses. His knowledge of horses was legendary, and he was a consummate horseman.

Jack's daughter Alison, co-editor of this book, had the immense foresight to carry out a series of taped interviews with her father, in his last years, and it is the transcripts of these tape-recordings that are the essence of his story – with a little help from his friends. And of friends Jack was enormously blessed. When he received an MBE in the 2002 Honours List 'for services to heavy horses', it was as if it had been given to the whole of the heavy horse fraternity. The respect in which he was held was demonstrated by the large number of people, from all over the country, who attended his funeral, two years later.

To read Jack's memories of a life in the farming community is to read a fascinating autobiography, but one coloured by real hardship. Although he was born as recently as 1920, it is to read a chapter of social history – of a constant battle to make ends meet. When his very young bride, and mother of his new baby, hobbled past the young man, working in the fields, it was because they could not afford new shoes for her. She was walking much further than she need, to save a penny ha'penny on her train fare. Jack most poignantly said: 'I don't mind admitting, I cried. I thought, what have we done to deserve this?'

But it was a life also of fun, and good-natured pranks, of which Jack was full. His close friends would not be surprised when the very passable old tramp begging for food round the show tents, gave them a knowing wink. It was also a life of 'making-do', and finding ingenious ways to solve problems cheaply. He was a family man, and a man who had deeply held principles of what was acceptable.

He would help anyone if he could. And Jack was always the same – however high or low the company he kept.

This story would have remained untold, had it not been for these detailed tapes, and the hours of dedicated transcribing that are the corollary of the taping. His memory, even with failing health, was astonishingly good.

It has been a pleasure to be involved in such a remarkable story, and to have had the opportunity of learning something about Jack Juby – horseman extraordinary.

Alan Childs
The Red House, Fakenham
July 2006

MAP SHOWING PLACES MENTIONED BY JACK JUBY

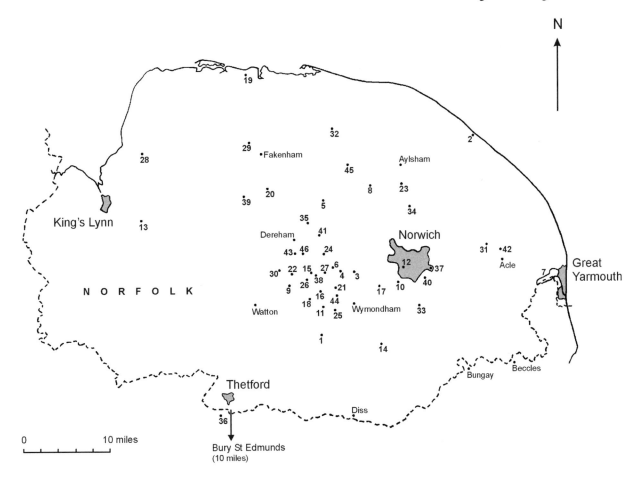

1	Attleborough	**24**	Mattishall
2	Bacton	**25**	Morley St Botolph
3	Barford	**26**	Reymerston
4	Barnham Broom	**27**	Runhall
5	Bawdeswell	**28**	Sandringham
6	Brandon Parva	**29**	Sculthorpe
7	Breydon Water	**30**	Shipdham
8	Cawston	**31**	South Walsham
9	Cranworth	**32**	Stody
10	Cringleford	**33**	Stoke Holy Cross
11	Deopham	**34**	Stratton Strawless
12	Earlham	**35**	Swanton Morley
13	East Winch	**36**	Thetford Heath
14	Forncett	**37**	Thorpe
15	Garvestone	**38**	Thuxton
16	Hardingham	**39**	Tittleshall
17	Hethersett	**40**	Trowse
18	Hingham	**41**	Tuddenham
19	Holkham	**42**	Upton
20	Horningtoft	**43**	Westfield
21	Kimberley	**44**	Wicklewood
22	Letton	**45**	Wood Dalling
23	Marsham	**46**	Yaxham

Jack in typical pose with his stallion and dog. He always had a dog with him.

1

EARLY YEARS

Jack Juby was born on 10 February 1920, into a farming community. His father was a council roadman or 'lengthman', working on the roads. His mother was a midwife, serving her neighbours in an untrained capacity. Jack was the eldest boy, and one of seven children, four boys and three girls. He remembered his first school, particularly the somewhat 'sparse' clothes he wore, and dinners that were rather 'do-it-yourself' affairs:

I started school when I was three and I went to Reymerston School. Today they would call it a kindergarten school. All we had to wear was a long pullover pulled between our legs, with a safety pin – that's how we went to school. We had old shoes and boots but no socks. With our packed dinner we used to take potatoes – hen's egg size – and the teacher put them under the old stove in the hot ashes. Then we'd have a hot potato for dinner, with a sandwich or whatever mother used to pack up – a bit of bread and jam or something.

Mrs Marjoram (I think that was her name) used to come from Norwich by train for the kindergarten school – plumpish woman. She used to walk from Thuxton to Reymerston. She was all right – she wasn't hard. She was more of a mother matron.

Always eager to help a member of the opposite sex, one afternoon at Reymerston school Jack gallantly offered his assistance to a scared young lady:

There was a thunderstorm – a really bad one. Eileen Stanford had got to go through the village down Silver Street and at least a mile across the old footpath up to Calveley Farm, and she was terrified. Me being the hero I've been all my life, I had to take Eileen home didn't I? Of course when I got to Calveley Farm and had escorted her home it was still thundering and lightening and I daren't come back home alone! But the cowman or yardman there, Mr Cook, who lived in a little old cottage in Reymerston, not far off North Green, had got to come home when he had finished his job, so I could come home with him. Anyhow Eileen's mother said to her husband (although I didn't know at the time – this came years later) 'if that little old boy has got to be about here I better give him something to eat.' Eileen said, 'I remember now my father said, "Don't you start feeding him do he'll come again!"' This conversation came about 70 years later, when I was in the insurance office in Hingham. We'd both done our business and I turned round and Eileen said, 'Well tha's Jack!' I said 'Yes. Tha's the gal Eileen!' Well we had a rare old conversation in there, and they all sat there listening. That was how I first started courting! In my eyes I was a hero, weren't I?

From Reymerston the young Jack moved to Garvestone School:

Then we went to Garvestone to Mrs Greenwood and Miss Tillett (before she got married). She came from Wymondham – smart young lady, so Jack thought. I liked her, she was all right, and she liked me. Anyway we used to have to touch our hat to her. She married Roy Shirras, and her mother and father had a fish shop in Wymondham.

But even with the attractions of Miss Tillett, school was something to be avoided if possible:

I've laid a-bed at North Green in that back bedroom. You can see right across the fields, and you can see Garvestone Church and Garvestone School. I've laid there when they have rung the first bell at five minutes to nine and then again at nine. I've gone across those fields half dressed, 10 minutes late, and got wrong for that. Then I'd nip home dinner-time and I wouldn't go back no more 'cos I got wrong at school! Or p'raps I wouldn't go home to North Green 'cos I would get wrong there. I'd go to the farm straightaway and I wouldn't go home till after school time. At the farm they'd say, 'What you up to, boy? You just going to give us a hand?' And I was happy again, weren't I?

Not surprisingly Jack's attention was drawn far more to what was happening in the fields and farms around his home than to the restrictive atmosphere of the classroom. He couldn't wait to escape, and of course in those early days it suited the farmers to have strong young lads helping at busy times of the year:

I didn't like school, and by the time I got to 11 years old, to go past the farm where the horses were – that was fatal! I used to dodge in there until it was too late to go to school. Then they'd give me a little something for helping. I used to lead the horses where they wanted them.

Springtime, when all the beet crop was growing in 20-inch rows, up and down, it was a job to keep the horses in the middle of those rows without jamming on the little plants. The men behind the horse-hoe, killing the weeds, had to keep in a direct line, or they would cut the little plants up, so they were glad of the boys to lead the horses up and down the rows all day long. They could get a permit from the council or school authority, for certain boys to have a day or two off to help them. I was always keen and interested, so I was always everybody's boy on the farm.

Young lad, believed to be Jack, sitting on a horse, helping on the farm. Lads like Jack were called 'howjee boys' because their signal to move on was when the men shouted 'Howjee'. This was a wonderful bit of old Norfolk meaning 'hold you tight', all run into one word.

Then that got to the middle of summer, or harvest-time, and there was all sorts of jobs that boys could do, like riding the horses to help the men who had the implements behind them. I was about 11 or 12 years old. Three or four days a week I'd be on different farms leading these horses about – that suited me better than school!

But in some ways the young Jack was perhaps in tune with the natural world around him, even if school didn't quite channel his talents:

I had to write an essay at school once, about the countryside. I reckon if I lay down on the ground I could hear the grass grow. That's the truth, and I wrote that when I grew up and became a man, I was going to cut down all the trees because it was the trees that made the wind blow. I had that in my head, but of course it was the wind that was blowing the trees.

There was a little 'vocational training' on offer for the older pupils:

We used to go to Thuxton Station once a week to go to Dereham School, for woodwork. One and a ha' penny fare from Thuxton Station to Dereham. As you go into Dereham the school on London Road, that's where it used to be. Woodwork for the boys, and cookery for the girls. The train was the 8.30 to Dereham them days. Nobody who worked on the farm never had watches – they didn't need them. They knew when every train went, like the 10 minutes to four. That would be the time to pull off the yoke and be going home.

Of course there were pranks and 'larks' to get up to, and in this respect Jack was never at a loss!

We used to have fun there – that used to keep us amused, but there wasn't any vandalism, like there is today. There was a row of little brick toilets – three and three. There were little old wooden seats and an old pail underneath. At the back of each little toilet they had a wooden door, which used to drop out, so when the cart came at night to empty the pails, they could pull them out of the back. Well, we used to have a game! You had to get a good old nettle – good thick stem – and drop the little door behind, so when the girls went into their toilet you could nip up behind. We used to know if we'd scored 'cos a little while later, when we all went into school and we sat down, if the one you tried to tickle up was uneasy on her seat – you'd scored!

With little money to spare, children's toys were simple ones, and children's pleasures were of the homespun variety:

A young Jack with his brother Bob on his back – a mischievous grin on both their faces!

As kids, we used to play out on the road. We used to make squares for hopscotch. Another big favourite was old bicycle wheels with the spokes out, and you'd have a stick in the rim. You could get them going and we used to race them. Mother used to have a whistle for us to go in when it was time. You could hear that all over the village. There would be a bit of bread and jam and then up the stairs to bed.

And their mother had her own way of making sure they stayed in bed!

Bed was about a quarter to seven. For years us three boys slept in one big bed behind the old chimney, with the curtain across, and mother used to tie us in with old fashioned long old scarves – tie them round us and then to the middle of the bed so we shouldn't fall out!

In the winter months there would be games indoors in the evenings – sometimes just rolling around on the floor, or sometimes playing tricks on each other. Jack's brother Raymond seemed always to be the ring-leader:

The games we used to play indoors! Mother and father had old high-armed chairs. Poor old father, he was deaf as a post. How mother ever managed I can't imagine. He used to sit with his pipe of 'bacca, and he used to go to sleep. That Raymond, he was always the ring-leader. He was naughty! We had a little old toy engine we used to wind up. One night Raymond crept up behind father and put it over top of his head to make him jump and 'course it caught all of his hair. 'Blast boy!' he used to shout! Then I remem-

Jack's brother Raymond.

ber one Saturday afternoon. I don't know how it happened but Raymond got a saucepan and stuck it on Peter's head with the handle out the back of his head, and he hammered it on. We couldn't get it off! Well there was panic there and Baker Burt came from Hingham. He came at six o'clock and he got some soapy water and got it off.

Jack also remembered a painful result of one of his brother's tricks!

We had an old toasting fork with three spikes and we used to have toast cooked over the fire. That is *really* toast when you do it like that. We used to have arguments about that and anyway something went wrong. I went to sit down and Raymond put the fork underneath the seat of my chair and I sat on that! All those little things amused us!

It seemed that Raymond didn't change at all. There was always something happening when he was around!

Poor old mother used to say, 'These hens, I've only got one egg again today.' He was taking an egg out of the run and taking it up the road. In the hedge he made a little nest so he'd get half a dozen eggs, he thought. He was going to get a

Jack feeding the pigs and chickens, watched by his brothers.

ha'penny for finding them, but of course they were mother's eggs weren't they! He was the one who used to yodel. You could hear him coming round the village. He went up to Watford later in life, and the bugger he got up and cart-wheeled down the street up on the pavement. He lived in Watford, but of course he was always a countryman at heart. He and a mate would go out on the bus to the country on Saturdays to go rabbiting. Well one Saturday he let a ferret out on the bus – on the top deck of the bus – and there weren't nobody looking. It upset all the people on the bus. This bloody ferret running about on the bus. He got his name in the papers. He'd rescued this ferret! You carried a ferret in your pocket in them days you see. You'd put the ferret in the hole and you'd hear it fluffing about underneath. You'd always have a dog, and he'd keep a looking. Then he'd go down the hole and get the rabbit.

In later years Jack biked to Watford to see his brother:

I'd go Thetford, Newmarket, Baldock, Royston, Stevenage – turn off the London road to the right. However I found my way I sometimes still wonder! It used to take anything from 10-12 hours. I'd have a bottle of water and a cheese sandwich. I'm not talking of Charles Dickens' time, I'm talking of myself. Sometimes brother Peter used to come back halfway with me, as far as Baldock, to keep me company. Then he would turn round and go back home again.

I come home one night and I had biked 122 mile. I went down the 'Buck' and had a pint, after I'd got home a little while.

Jack played a bit of football, and there was one 'needle' match he remembered that ended in his team taking their revenge on a whole community!

I can remember we had a football team – 11 of us. We used old coats and things for the goal posts and we got up a team and we went to Mattishall Burgh. We used to go down Town Lane over the bridge. We were the big team! You talk about Manchester City and Norwich City! We lost 11-0 and we were so riled we came all the way back on the back roads. Nearly everyone had goats and rabbit hutches then. The little bit better-off would have a pony and cart. Well, we came all that way home through Town Lane and we let the goats off and turned the rabbit hutches upside down and we took people's gates off the hinges – all the way home. That was our revenge for losing 11-0. But they weren't bad things like they do today. That was the process of growing up, and of course anything like that Jack had to be there!

And he was certainly 'there' if a bit of mischief was to be had in the village shop:

Where Kathleen Shirras' shop is now, that is where Mr Softley used to be – a biggish sort of man. We were in there one day doing a bit of scheming. They had sweets in big glass jars. One of the boys said he wanted a blue spinning top instead of a red top, so Mr Softley went into the back of the shop to change it. Whilst he was gone I whipped the top off the jar and grabbed a handful of sweets. But the only thing was, my hand was full and the top of the jar was narrow. But no way was I going to let go of the sweets!

But there was always summary justice in the form of the village bobby – an institution lamented by many!

'Course there was the village policeman (on a bicycle) in those days, if you were naughty. But they were alright. What the old policeman would sometimes do, if you were naughty, he'd catch hold of you, give you a good telling-off and then he'd get hold of your ear and twist it. You'd scream 'cos you thought it was going to come off. And then he stuck his toe up your arse! We used to get wrong for things, like we weren't allowed to go into certain woods to get chestnuts, 'cos we'd break the branches off the trees. Well they might as well have told us to go and do it mightn't they! The policeman caught us once and he got hold of my jersey. Then he twisted my ears and stuck his foot into my backside. Later he told my mother, (who was delivering papers then) and she said to him, 'He didn't tell me.'
'No,' replied the policeman, 'He said he wouldn't let anybody know.' I was a big boy and I wasn't going to blah to mother. I could be doing the same thing today and they would take me to court and I could go to court and brag about it. But I didn't brag about his making me howl, did I? He used to twist your lugs and you'd scream, and stick his toe up your backside and he'd say, 'Perhaps you've larnt your lesson.' Now that was a good way of keeping you under control.

Animals of course were part of Jack's upbringing and part of his love of life, as well as a means of finding food:

I always had dogs – I can't remember not having a dog. Mind you everybody had dogs. They were always kept outside – all sorts of kennels and all sorts of dogs – mongrels most of them. The Howes boys once clipped all the hair off the sheepdog and then sold it to the local policeman as a greyhound! We three boys used to go down to Mr Howes to have a hair cut. Sixpence for the three of us. He used to sit the dog in front of us so we daren't move! With ferrets and dogs we used to go and get rabbits. If a dog went up the roadside and you see his old tail a-going and he'd be excited and scrapping at the ground – there'd be a rabbit. So we used to get the old rose briars that have inch hooks on them and put one down the hole and pull it out, and there would be fur on it. And it was warm, so you'd put it back again and twist it and you'd get hair and their skin. Then you'd pull the rabbit out, kill it on the back of the neck, pull out the guts and in the pan it would go. This is not a fairy tale, nor 100 years ago. This was out of desperation. Threepence a skin off the old rag and bone man, and white meat – lovely. When we were kids at home, we used to argue over whose turn it was to eat the eyes! Mother used to put the whole thing in the pot, head and all, then she'd add split peas and Norfolk dumplings, that sort of thing. That was real meat.

Their father was a council roadman, and Jack enjoyed helping him when he could:

My father he was a lengthman on the roads, trimming the hedges and the sides of the roads –the skirtings they used to call it – to keep that all level along the road, and clean the potholes up. There used to be a firm in Shipdham then – they were the contractors with their lorries. They used to order a load of stuff (road materials) to come. Father used to put sticks here and sticks there all round the village where he wanted them to unload a little of this stuff. He used to go with his barrow and broom and keep sweeping it in, to keep the potholes full.

In the wintertime, when it was frosty weather, he'd be up early. He'd be gone by six o'clock. When there was a sharp frost he'd have his wheelbarrow and a rope round his neck so he could take the weight. He'd have his one (free) hand and he'd have his shovel and he'd keep spreading the sand where the ice was. He'd do the whole village – different places. He had to do round the school gates to keep the kids from sliding about. He'd do outside the post-office and the shops. He'd always sprinkle at the Rectory – outside their gates. He'd get an ounce of tobacco or something at Christmas time! So he looked after the hot-shots in the village. He'd have it all done by 10 o'clock.

In the winter snow – 'cos we used to *get* snow then – all along North Green it used to drift up against the hedges. Igloos we used to call it. We used to dig little basins in and they were our little homes. The farmer down the road – Stanley Mortlock – had horses. He had the council supply different villages, or different 'distances'. My father's distance was part of Hardingham, all of Reymerston and part of Garvestone. That was the 'length' he had to keep in charge of. The snow-plough was allocated to Mortlock by the council, and father had to go out with two horses and try to keep the snow off the road. He had a big wooden sledge thing and that had a point with a big iron (like a ship) at the front. It would open and shut, and you had to put the two horses on the front of that and drive the horses through the snow, and that could make a nice big path. 'Course I had to go down first thing in the morning and help father with his lantern to feed the horses and get them ready, and we'd be gone before daylight, clearing the roads of snow.

Because of his father's deafness Jack often accompanied him to act as his spokesman:

Jack's father John, back row left, with Jack on the far right (c. late 1930s).

Another little thing that always sticks in my mind, every Thursday night I used to have to go with my father to Yaxham – through Reymerston across the footpath over the main road past the church, down Town Lane over the bridge and across the footpath. That was where his governor lived (the one above father). He had a little old motorbike and side chair. Father used to go there with his time-sheet to get his money, and 'course Jack he had to go. I always use to toddle along. Where he went I had to go. I was his interpreter. I don't know none of the others went, it was always me.

They had a little old terrier dog. His wife would always give me a cake when they were seeing to their business and I would always give the dog a bit of this cake, and I used to get wrong! When I got home mother used to say that was rude – the woman gave me the cake and I would give the dog a bit of it. I could never see through that one. I thought I was being rude and greedy *not* to patronize the little dog? Now how do you weigh that one up? Who was right and who was wrong? Well, there's no end of things in life like that in bigger ways and in more different ways. You have to do what you think is right and somebody else will think that that is wrong!

His father would do any job to earn a little more money:

He used to dig gardens for people – acres and acres of garden. Miss Goff had a big long garden next door and he took that over. She had all she wanted out of it. He'd go round after tea at night, mowing meadows for hay for people.

Jack's father John Juby, outside the row of cottages known as North Green, Reymerston, with buckets of water from the well.

The lack of money was a constant worry for families in the villages, and especially when doctors' bills occurred.

The doctor had to be paid for – that's one thing I'll always remember, it sticks in my mind. Poor old mother she had her money ready. Oh God, she had to lay out. She had it all counted out: so much for the baker, so much for the grocery man (Mr Shirras when he came), so much for the butcher. And it would all be worked out to the ha' penny. I always remember my poor old mother crying like anything one morning. She'd got a letter through the post. I couldn't understand all the rigmarole but she was wholly upset. She had got a bill from Dr James of Hingham for one of us boys who'd had pneumonia or something, and that would have been about £2 something. That was something out of the blue she hadn't budgeted for, and that used to worry her a lot as she would never have wanted to owe anybody anything. I can remember that I couldn't make out why she was so upset.

Despite being so 'hard up' Christmas was of course very special, and Jack's mother always managed to prepare a wonderful meal for her family:

Cottage at North Green Reymerston, where Jack was born. Grandmother Alice Juby, with one of her daughters.

Ever since I can remember, at Christmas, one of my sisters – I suppose that would be the eldest one Edna – she always used to plan her week from London, for Christmas. We had a good Christmas dinner – mother always managed a good Christmas dinner – but presents and things, we didn't have presents like they do today. But they always managed to fill our stockings with something. We would have an orange in the bottom, an apple, a little parcel of nuts and a little parcel of seeds. And the main thing we used to have was the old things you used to blow, and a streamer would go out. That was Christmas. We'd probably go down to grandfather's in Silver Street in the afternoon to see how they got on. I can't remember them coming to ours.

Of his father's large family, Jack could remember some of his relatives:

Aunt Rose was fat and Uncle Jim was thin: they lived out Stowmarket way. Aunt Lil, Aunt Maud, Aunt June, Aunt May and Aunt Kate, Uncle Will and Uncle John – there were several of them. They were all brought up in Reymerston and drifted away, but father was born and lived and died in Reymerston. They used to pay about £2 a year rent, or something like that. They used to pay Mr Fuller, who was a bit of a builder and decorator, and the cottage belonged to him. There used to be such an argument. They wanted a new door sometime but that would take about two years rent to pay for the bloody door. I always remember thinking that! Mr Fuller used to come round with a bit of clay and patch up a few holes and such like.

And very special to Jack of course was his grandfather, who was a farm-labourer and lived in the same village:

Sometimes on a Sunday evening in the summer we'd go down to Silver Street and see my granny and grandad, and we'd have bread and butter and jam sandwiches, then as a big treat, a bit of her homemade cake. That was something!

Jack remembered the old man's cottage very clearly – and especially the sanitary arrangements:

Grandfather lived in the cottages at the bottom of Silver Street, in one of the two cottages. William Scase lived next door. He was a carpenter and he used to make coffins. He made my grandfather's coffin and it cost five pounds for an oak coffin with brass handles. Us and the boy Scases and the boy Perfects were all about the same age, but of course I was always so forward I would always be with the older ones.

If you had gone round the corner of the cottage by the back door you would have seen there was an old nail stuck up there and that is where we used to hang the creepers on. They were irons with hooks on and there were three of them. The hooks would be upwards and a pole in the middle with a ring on, and you'd tie that to a linen line or a plough-end, anything that was strong enough, and you push that right down the well. That would catch the pail you had lost! You'd bring two or three pails up sometimes, that people had lost down the well. Kids would sometime come and borrow them when they had lost a pail down the well.

Down the bottom of the garden was the closet and that was a three-seater – two big ones and a little one on the end. It had a trap door at the back and that had a hole that went out the back that would be covered over with wood, and the sludge went down there. Once a year grandad used to have to pull the wood all up and have a long pole with a ladle-type saucepan on the end, and dig a hole in the garden and bury all that. I often wonder what George (sister Hilda's husband) used to think when they came down from London for the weekend! That bloody old toilet round the back there, it stunk like hell, and was full of flies. Little square pieces of newspaper as well! We didn't know any different did we? That was nothing to us.

We used to have our own path and then there was the middle path, which was communal. Uncle Will had his path with the big gate to let his pony and cart in. Down the side of our path was a big ditch. In the house Hilda modernised a stove so mother could cook on a Valor paraffin stove, 'cos before, she used to cook on the old fire. You'd have an oven in the wall in one corner and the copper up the other.

Jack's sister Hilda and his mother Alice outside the North Green cottage.

Jack's grandfather and grandmother, James and Harriet Juby. They lived in Silver Street, Reymerston.

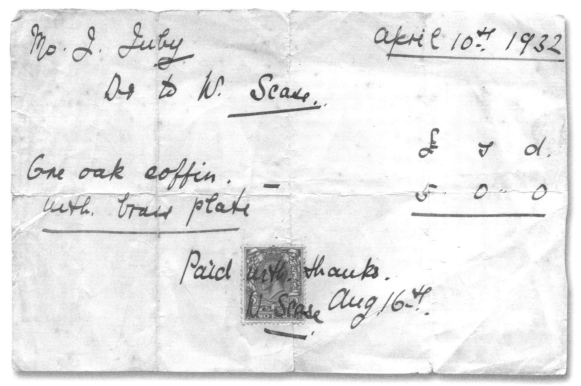

Original receipt from a local carpenter for a coffin, believed to be for Jack's grandfather, dated 10 April 1932.

Jack's father and mother, John and Alice Juby.

Jack remembered his parents as 'strict church':

My mother – I can picture her now. That bring tears to my eyes every time I think about it. She wasn't a very big woman and father he was a big tall man. He couldn't do much only join in with what he thought, because he was deaf. But mother she could go to any church service and stand there. I'm proud of it. There wasn't a hymn or psalm she needed a book for.

And young Jack spent a good deal of his time in church as well.

I went to Reymerston Church several times a week, on a Sunday, Wednesday night and all choir practices. All weddings and funerals I had to go to church for pumping the organ. Blowing the organ that had an old handle like a blacksmith's bellows and a little old weight hung on the lead. It used to come up and down, and when that come right up you were empty. The harder he played, the harder you had to pump, but when you got the weight down that meant you could have a breather. That was when I used to wink and put my thumbs up to the girls in the choir! I was hid up behind there and I could see them.

But Jack also learned how to ring the bells and sometimes had to combine the two jobs – with some difficulty!

I can go and do it now: 1-2-3, 1-2-3, one in my foot 1-2-3, 1-2-3, 1-2-3, 'come to church, come to church.' Then you'd finish up. The last minute the curate would give you the down, you'd got to pull one bell. I used to have to pull that about six times then I had to run across to the organ and start pumping that, so he could play the introduction music. I done that for eight years, three times on a Sunday.

Jack remembered that the church and village outings were often combined. He enjoyed these until he was 'shopped' for being a paid employee!

We used to have the school outing and village outing once a year on Shirras' bus. The school outing and church outing combined and they would have a bus load go to Yarmouth. We used to have our little spade and pail and a stick of rock and have a day out in Yarmouth. After a year or so, some of the knowledgeable people found out I was getting a pound a year for ringing the bells at Reymerston and I wasn't allowed to go on the outings anymore! Later on I did do a bit of bell ringing – not just the chimes – and I wished I had kept it up. The only wedding I got involved in with that form of bell-ringing was when Captain Hare from Reymerston Hall got married to the parson's daughter.

Jack still remembered vividly his father's last illness:

I shall never forget just before father died at North Green – he'd got bronchial pneumonia and they'd got him on a gas cylinder. He kept pulling his collar. He was a big fellow and I sat aside his bed. I'll never forget that he was the most determined man you ever met. They used to wear these thick shirts, right down to your knees and a collar with studs. He sat trying to undo his collar. He was trying to get his breath and was trying to undo his bloody collar. He cursed and I knew exactly what he wanted. I went to get hold of it but he pushed me out of

Jack's parents' Golden Wedding held at North Green: back row (l–r): Bob, Raymond, Peter, Jack, Olive; front row (l–r) Hilda, Alice, John and Edna.

the way and that was the last thing he ever done. He'd been in bed several days but he never had a wet patch or nothing in the bed. The most independent man all his life.

Jack's mother performed the duties of midwife to her community:

Mother she was a midwife, although she wasn't trained. There were very few trained midwives in those days. It was something she started and things snowballed from there. She used to perform her duties for Reymerston, Garvestone, Thuxton and Yaxham. The miles that little woman has biked. Some of the cases she had to take on for Dr James. She had to look after them for 10 days, coming home in the evenings to see to us children, then returning. Sometimes they wouldn't need her all the time.

My mother was also an agent for Kay's catalogue, getting orders for all sorts of things for you. She had a box on the back of her bike. She also used to lay people out. She was the hardest working woman ever. *Her* mother and father used to have a little business in Hethersett and they used to drive a cart to Norwich everyday, with butter and eggs, and have a stall in Norwich.

Jack's mother Alice with her sister Daisy.

And of course, in those early days in the country, everything was delivered by horse and cart – to Jack's little world of the 'six cottages' – the neighbouring houses he remembered so well:

Milk was delivered by cart and the butcher had a horse and cart. Burt the baker from Hingham, he used to come round with a high-boxed cart with the bread. He used to tie his horse up by the gate and used to come down by the path and do the six cottages. There used to be someone come round on a bike with a tray on the front selling ice-cream. You used to get a ha' penny cornet or a penny for a wafer. If you got one of them in a week you were lucky.

Below: Mr Frost, a butcher from Hingham, with Jack's grandmother Harriet.

Below, right: A family group at North Green: back row, father John, Edna and mother Alice; front row: Jack, Peter, Bob and Raymond.

We lived in the end cottage. Then Miss Goff, a spinster – she was a tailor for the Hall and the parson. Next down was Mrs Adcock – she was a widow woman. Then Uncle Will and Aunt Maud. Uncle Will was brother to my father – they had the same size family as we did – seven children – and they lived there all their married lives in those old houses. Next door to Uncle Will was Mr and Mrs Isbell, and on the end was the biggest house out of the six – that had a little barn and out-buildings and that was Mr and Mrs Ward. He had two biggish ponies and he used to do a bit of ploughing and have a bit of land.

Jack's mother Alice and his brother Bob at Thuxton station.

And like his brothers and sisters, Jack was prepared to take his place in this predictable world, once his obligations to education were over:

There were four boys and three girls. The girls used to go into service at the age of 14. We all left school at 14 and the girls went to London to go into service. I don't know what connection there was, but think an aunt and uncle in London took the girls in – 'service skivvies' they called them.

A big thing was when my sisters used to come home by train from London for a weekend or whatever, once a year or something like that. We all used to walk down to Thuxton Station to meet them off the train. They'd bring a bar of choco-late – that was something!

One of the three sisters, Edna, gained a good appointment in the Rothschild household and this led to a memorable visit to London for Jack:

Edna spent a lot of her years with Lord Rothschild and that's where we went for King George V's Jubilee. I never can remember how we got there – by train I suppose. My father took me to London and we were on Lord Rothschild's balcony 'cos they were away at the time. We were up there and we could see the whole procession. I had a brown double-breasted long trouser suit – my first – bought on purpose to see King George V's Jubilee! How mother and father paid for that, my first little suit to wear, I don't know! I suppose it was my sisters helped. We stayed there and 'course that was something in those days. I had never seen anything like it.

Even while still at school, Jack had been accepted by the adults around him. Stanley Mortlock had been one of a number of farmers only too eager to employ this strong young boy who was so willing to learn. And Jack even had to be ready to act as 'knocker-up' to his boss!

Stanley, he would not get up in the morning. He'd say, 'Have yer fed Smiler, have yer fed so and so? Well, looks as if they are cleaned out', (meaning they have eaten it all up). Then we'd have to yoke up and go onto work, go ploughing or harrowing somewhere and I'd go with him. After a round or two he let me have a go harrowing with the harrows: 'You can manage them now boy, I'll just go into the yard and do something', and he would leave me there. For an hour I was king of the castle weren't I? Bugger school and the old school bell. I could hear them kids shrieking out there to play. I was happier than they were. In the afternoon I used to get tired,

Jack's father John with Jack and his sister Hilda attending King George V's Silver Jubilee in London. Note Jack's suit!

then he used to hull his old coat down on the bank and say to me, 'You'd better have a minute or two there boy.' I'd go sound asleep for an hour, then away I'd go again. I just couldn't be away from it. I got so in my little way, after about a year, I was doing a man's work, 'cos I enjoyed it so much and it was nothing to me. Even up until two years ago no day was too long and no work was too hard 'cos I enjoyed what I was doing and like to keep busy!

So before leaving school Jack had already made a start in the world of work, and at 14 there was the escape from the classroom that he had wanted. The next stage of his life was to begin, and he was excited by the prospect.

STARTING WORK

Stanley Mortlock had been one of a number of farmers well used to 'employing' the young schoolboy for a few pence, and was an obvious employer when Jack eventually left school:

I started working at Stanley Mortlock's farm at Reymerston – feeding the pigs, and learning to milk the cows. I could milk when I was 14 year old. Cor, I used to enjoy that milking – that used to be some old game. You used to get a penny in your hand and you should be able to strip a cow out without losing that penny. So you were gentle weren't you – between your thumb and finger. I loved it! You'd have an old pail between your knees and the froth would come up lovely!

Stanley only had three cows. He used to churn the milk and make butter in a big old churn that would go round and round. Then it would go lumpy and that was a-thickening-up and that would all come up along the top and then make that into butter. That *was* butter. That had got some taste about it.

Stanley also kept pigs, but the creature Jack remembered especially was a fierce old turkey:

I was always busy and happy – always happy. I remember an old stag turkey – I killed an old stag turkey. He'd chase yer and come after yer, his old wings out – he'd really mean it! He chased me one day and I ran to get in the door – a little old front door we used to get in the house. I ran in there, banged the front door and I got his head through. I hung onto the door and he broke his neck! That put paid to him. He was a dangerous old b.... When he chased you his old head went bright red. I reckoned he committed suicide!

Travelling up to Norwich to the cattle market became a regular part of Jack's life.

When I worked for Stanley Mortlock I used to go up the cattle market every Saturday with the horse and cart. In real bad weather we used to have to tie the horses' feet in and wrap their feet in hessian sacking. We used to cut out a foot and a half square of hessian and set their foot on it, then bring it up around the ankle and fetlock, and tie it round there. That would get us half way to Norwich, on a Saturday. Then we'd pull in at Barford 'Cock', jump down and pull the old sacks off and put another lot on. That would stop them slipping on the ice and snow. We used to go up the cattle market on the hill. You'd go to your respective unloading place with whatever you'd got on, and stand behind the horse. Stanley used to say, 'Hang onto them shafts, boy, hang onto them shafts, boy!'

You see when they were pulling something heavy off the back of the cart, the shafts would go up and that would sometimes upset the old horse so they'd snap at yer or bite yer! Then they'd stable the horse. There were stables about there then that're now turned into garages. We'd put the horse into the stable and turn the cart up and go about your day dealing – whatever you had to do. I'm talking about the market on the hill, the one that was near the castle then.

Even at this early age Jack was interested in horses, and is here shown 'picking up' the horse's feet.

Jack as a young lad with a horse.

Stanley never knew when he was going to be needed to transport something back to an isolated farm, so Jack's hours were also very unpredictable:

When we used to come home on a Saturday night after the market, different farmers would have come up and say, 'I've got a calf in them pens there – could you bring that home for me?' Well, that was Stanley Mortlock's business. Old Henry Abbott (?), the forerunner of Abbott Brothers, he'd got a crate of this, or he'd got an old goose and – could we take that home? You'd tie the legs of the goose and set that in the bottom of the cart. You used to have all sorts of things under your seat in the cart, netted over top.

There was this cattle dealer from Swanton Morley – he'd come onto the farms and try and buy something from you or sell you something. He was a general cattle dealer and one day he bought this half a dozen cattle and he wanted to get them home to Dereham, to his 'dumping paddock', we used to call it! He'd get them down there and then during the week he'd sort them out. He'd either put some more with them or get another farmer to come and have a look at them, and sell them to him during that week – earn a pound a piece out of them. That was his living. Anyhow we'd brought one load of stuff home, a crate of rabbits and that sort of thing, and then we had to put another horse in the cart and go back again to get these cattle out of the pens and drive them home to Dereham – down past Barford 'Cock', then onto Skipping Block Corner and Hardingham.

On the journey home, Jack's usual job was to make sure gates to the houses and cottages were closed, so the animals did not stray into the gardens:

'Course in them days there was nothing like the amount of houses there is now. They were scattered about then. You'd see a pair of cottages and then you'd go two or three mile afore you'd see another pair, so we knew the gateways and the crossroads when we left Norwich. You left Earlham Hill and then you'd be in the clear for a long way. I'd jump in the cart and ride behind the cattle then. All of a sudden Stanley would say, 'You'd better get out boy and get them gates in front of them cottages.'

He could see the cottages perhaps half a mile away and I used to have to nip in front of the cattle and then go and do them gates up, and stand there to make sure the cattle went past. Then I'd jump in the cart again and the next one would be perhaps near Barford 'Cock' and I'd jump out, run along the side past the cattle and stand in the gateway. We used to come all that way home to Dereham and turn them out on that little old paddock down the hill. By this time it was getting dark and then we'd jump into the cart and ride home from Dereham through Garvestone, and he'd drop me off at North Green.

One night I went tearing off down the yard, 'cos I was late:
'Cor!' mother say to me, 'Your father's been up and down that road two or three times after you. He's going to give you a hiding! Be you a-getting upstairs to bed out of the way,' she said. And she bundled me off up the stairs to bed.
When father came in he say, 'I can't see him.'
'No,' she say, 'Tha's because you hen't been looking! He's been upstairs asleep in bed all the time.'

Well anyway that saved me a bloody thrashing, 'cos he was worried and upset you see, and about my payment for that day.

But payment at this stage of his career was not always as Jack, or his dad, expected:

Old Stanley, as he dropped me off at the gate he say, 'You've done well boy. I'll give you an egg when the hens lay!'

So keen was the young boy however, to do the work he loved, Jack would even turn up for duty in the evenings:

Friday nights I'd go down there waiting, and perhaps Stanley would take a couple of calves out to Barnham Broom, or Brandon Parva, or to some other farmers. They'd have bought some pigs and all sorts of things. You'd maybe take a calf, put in a sack, with its head out, and tied in there. When you got there you'd cut the string and let it out. They had to be delivered by horse and cart. Everything was done with horse and cart – after tea on a Friday night!

But Jack was part of Stanley's great move to motorised transport:

One of Stanley's sisters, Eva, somewhere along the line married a Londoner, Ted Dawson. Ted got Stanley fixed up with a lorry – little old Ford – with cushion tyres blown up hard at the front, and hard ones at the back. Single wheels – only a little old thing. That used to go with a 'connector coil'. Half a dozen of these little old coils on the dashboard, I should imagine. That had a gate change and only two gears, two forwards. The reverse you used to have to use the handbrake.

Well anyhow, this little lorry, we cut the back off and made it into a truck. We put high sides on it, bars across the top, put the back in and made a cattle float. The back-board unfolded in two, and we used to put ash poles in – shove them and tie them underneath the chassis and pull them out when you wanted to use the tailboard. When we was up Norwich we used to have to watch out 'cos we'd got these poles underneath the lorry, and people used to pinch them for firewood. That was my job, to keep an eye on them.

Well, that lorry was modern in them days – this was when I was about 14. Cor, that used to be something. You used to sit in there and the driver had the wheel a foot and half from his side. I could sit in the other side and use the hooter. It was a box concern and you had a handle on it. You could pull it up and down and that was my job to operate that.

Once we had to go to Stoke Holy Cross. Well that was the other side of the world weren't it, in them days – the other side of Norwich, to pick up a couple of little Jersey heifers. Anyhow some kids on Trowse hill were running alongside of us wanting to know if we wanted a push, we were going so slow!

The unenviable job of getting his boss up in the mornings continued, but Jack's ploys became more subtle:

Well that got so Saturday morning we'd got two load to do. 'You'll have ter call me up, boy,' Stanley said. Poor old mother she had to get *me* up by half past four, and at a quarter to five I'd go tearing off to Mortlock's. I'd milk two old cows perhaps, time I was waiting for him. I kept shouting up to his windows. The bugger he would *not* get up and it was my responsibility, in my mind weren't it, to get him up early enough to go to Norwich? Oh dear! Then I got so I could start the motor up. That was when I beat him. You'd have to get the back axle up, jack that off the ground, put it into gear and then crank it. When I got that going and backed that across the yard, he'd hear that a-going. I was burning petrol then, weren't I! He'd get out of bed then. Perhaps the next week I'd turn it round ready to go. I got ever so clever. I'm talking when I was fourteen, and that was near 70 year ago.

The conversion job, making their lorry into a cattle float, was not without its problems. They fell foul of government regulations:

There were Ministry regulations then and word got round that Stanley'd got to take it and get it weighed because they wanted to charge more tax for the cattle float. To get that under weight we got Mr Scase the local carpenter (he had a business in the village making coffins and gates and such like) to come down there the night before we had to go up to Dereham to have it weighed. We knew it was going to be over-weight, and Mr Scase took all the floor boards out. We went to Dereham that next morning and there was a Ministry man, a weighbridge man and a policeman, and we went onto a little old weighbridge. They weighed in halves. They put a chalk mark on the side and they weighed it in halves – they still do that sort of thing today. Anyway we got it underweight and come home again and put the floor boards back!

And the old lorry was so temperamental that genuine 'horse power' had often to be used!

We'd get a ton of sugar beet on that little old lorry cart to Thuxton station and into trucks. Bloody hard work chucking that up into those trucks. Like when we was going to cart Stanford's beet up from mile road. They'd cart it off the field and tip it up on the side of the road so we could cart it to the station – a little haulage job. We were going to do that but the times we have gone there, loaded up the beet and the lorry wouldn't start up! 'You'll have to go and get Old Smiler and put the traces on him, boy.' I'd go and get Smiler and I've hung onto the front of the old lorry and gone past North Green down to Thuxton Station, pulled up against the truck, chucked the beet off into the truck and the bloody thing would start up and we'd drive home then. That was the first cattle float.

There was always a little bit of scheming going on with village animals, and Jack was of course always willing to help.

We kept pigs and cows and when the cow was in season, that was when I used to have to go back after dark and sneak round the village and let the old cow in the field with a local farmer's bull. I've also gone down the road with an old sow, past the houses, and let the old pig in with somebody else's boar at night – got her serviced, we did! But I loved that life. And we still kept horses to work on the farm.

Just occasionally sheer tiredness caught young Jack out. He remembers well the painful consequences of one lapse of concentration:

Everybody had allotments then – all the parish – and different people would get Stanley to go and plough their half-acre with his horse. Where the Reymerston roundhouse is, we used to plough four allotments there on that corner. They've gone now. We were there once and Stanley had got a colt on the plough. He used to say 'touch him up, boy', and you had to be quick to touch him up otherwise he wanted to stop, and if not he'd jump up you see. I was tired and I was toddling along behind him in the furrow half asleep and the colt ploughed into a wasp nest in the middle of that field, and I fell into it and that stung me all over. I was in a pickle! Mother, she soaked the old-fashioned blue bags and softened them up and plastered them all over me. Even then it didn't stop me. I had to go again the next day.

Jack remembers a local accident at this time, quite clearly:

One Friday we came out of Dereham – that was the West Dereham Railway then – and there was such a commotion at the railway crossing. Something had happened. The Mays (?) brothers – they farmed up at Carlick (?) Farm at Garvestone – had got what we call a bit of a 'blood mare'. She'd got a bit of blood in her. Nasty old bastard she was. She'd run away and hit the gates and shot them out of the cart.

Anyway Stanley bought the old mare and took it off and I had to ride in the back of the cart and lead the old mare home behind our cart. The first thing he did when we got home was set about her. He got me onto her back and she got away. I went right down the bottom of them fields, down at Richardson's meadows, and she got stuck in an old thorn hedge. She got stuck in there and tha's where they come and rescued me. Cor, I was a- screaming and howling. I was frightened weren't I, something frightened. But I hung onto her right down the bottom of those fields. She was an old bastard she was, but Stanley broke her in the finish.

And it seems that Stanley often succeeded where others had failed:

There used to be a place in Dereham (on the left near Baxter Row) where people used to school horses. We've had them away from there what they couldn't do anything with. Stanley used to go and get a horse away from there, tie it to the back of the horse and cart and bring it home. He used to put a lot of work in to get them right.

Jack was still learning his trade of course, and sometimes things went badly wrong:

We come home from Norwich after the second load one Saturday morning. I shall never forget that 'cos didn't I get wrong! A cob stood in the cart with a lump of green stuff out of his mouth. He'd got the bridle on and the old bit in his mouth and he weren't enjoying that 'cos he couldn't eat it how he liked. Well I thought I'd get that bit off his mouth and he'd enjoy that a little better. So I undone the buckle to take the bridle off, to let the bit out, and of course the blinkers were gone and then he could see the bloody cart and the wheels behind him. Blast, he took off up the yard through them gates. There was a great old high hedge and he got in a muddle. He got in there but that was as far as he could go. Cor, didn't I get wrong – and we had to go back to Norwich again that day.

Stanley Mortlock, his boss, would turn everything into an opportunity for making a little money:

People would have a dead ewe or dead calf and they'd get onto Stanley and want it out of the way, and he used to go and pick that up. He'd skin it, then sell the skin or the fleece or whatever it was. Then round the back of the barn he'd have a copper built in there and a stove and grating underneath, and we used to boil the meat up – boil it all up and feed the pigs with it. I used to have to stir it up and if it was too thick put some more water with it, and then take a couple of pails and put them into the pig-sty. He used to say 'keep that old fire a-going, boy, keep that old fire a-going.'

But even Stanley allowed an animal to get the better of him occasionally:

As you go down Hardingham Low Street, there's a farm up there. We used to go up a track there, to a gentleman farmer who had a farm at Runhall and a farm at the Grove. He'd got an old ewe lay up there he wanted cleared up. Where you get livestock you get deadstock, no matter whether it's chickens, rabbits or pigs or whatever – you'll always get some dead. There's nothing wrong with that.

Well, we had got to go down to Runhall Farm to pick something up from there and then turn right out of the gate. Well the old mare, she knew that coming out of there there's some iron railings round that corner. Stanley was trying to get her to go right and she was determined she was going to the left. She got hung up on the railings and chucked the old sheep out of the cart onto the road. There was a blacksmith's shop up the road and we rescued her out of the railings and we led her up the road to the blacksmith's shop. Stanley heated up a poker and put it into the side of her mouth. She'd got what we call a hard old mouth. She wouldn't respond to the bit – but of course there weren't the bits about then like there are today. But then he could pull the reins how he wanted them.

From the time that Jack started working for Stanley Mortlock, he was well aware that his Union was fighting his corner for him, and although strike action was not something that Jack could accept, nevertheless his gratitude for what the Union had achieved was deep-felt:

I was about 13 years old when I was first helping Stanley Mortlock, then when I got to 14, I was full-time on the farm. I suppose I got about half a crown a day or something about that. When I got married at 16 and went to Deopham, a full man's wages then was 30 shillings in old money – that was standard. The first rise in agricultural wages in my life-time was when the Union fought and fought and they got us one and sixpence a week rise. That was a lot of money then. After about two year there was another appeal for farm workers' wages and that went up three and sixpence. You weren't allowed to work after 11 o'clock on a Saturday morning. They took an hour off the week's working time – which was the law. That was something weren't it! I'm not an advocator of unions and strikes and that sort of thing.

I never did believe in that. That was a poor answer I think, but I also stuck to the Union. I have been a life member since I was 60 – a free life member. Because father was a staunch union man he put us boys in the Union as soon as we earned money, so we kept it up like that. My argument is, I didn't demand one and sixpence rise in that year. I didn't go to the fight and argue – because we daren't. So the Union got us that didn't they? That was my Union that got us three and sixpence rise later on, and that hour off a week. My respect for the Union is because *we* weren't strong enough *or* brave enough to do it ourselves. But in regards to these strikes – they make me sick! That isn't the answer. There's a compromise somewhere, isn't there?

Sometime much later on, at Lime Tree Farm, Jack recalls another union issue:

See, on the farm one year, a lot of years ago, there was 12 of us – 11 and my son 'Tarzan' (Kenny), a 16-year-old. We used to line up Friday night four o'clock, bicycles against the hedge, in that little passage-way, to go and get our money – one at a time. When the money went up again, one man would not be in the union. He was strongly against it you see. We had such arguments about that on the farm. The Union was fighting for another two pound or something like that, so I said to that man in the gang going up to the door, I said, 'I want you to go first. You go first look, and you refuse to take that rise and I'll shake hands with you.' If he was that much against the union he should have refused it and said, 'No, I'll fight my own battles.' But he accepted anything the union got for him, didn't he? That was wrong. I always thought that was wrong.

So life in rural Norfolk was changing in all sorts of ways but Jack wondered whether it was for the best:

It's frightening to see how things have progressed – but have they progressed? That was the way of life and people were happy. You had time to shout and talk to one another when you were going along with the horse and cart. You'd see someone across the hedge and you'd have a conversation with them as you were going past, but you don't do that now. Everybody knew everybody. It's indescribable some times to see how things have changed – tractors and one thing and another. I sometimes wonder if things have changed for the better.

A FAMILY MAN

Whilst still a teenager, a young lady entered Jack's life, and things were soon to change forever:

I worked for Stanley Mortlock 18 months to two year I suppose. In that time I met mother (Margaret), who was a maid. All 14 and 15-year old girls were in service. She came from Bawdeswell. The big farmers at Bawdeswell – the Edmintons (?) – were good Chapel people and they looked after the poor and needy in Bawdeswell. That is what mother's family were! They had butter, eggs, milk and little bits of leftovers. It was the Edmintons who knew Captain Hare at Reymerston Hall and they knew he needed another maid, so they got mother into Reymerston Hall. That is how we first met. We met going to choir practice. Being up at the hall she had to be in the choir and I was blowing the organ weren't I? After church was over I used to take them (mother and the other maid) back to the Hall – see them home safe and sound. I don't know who fell in love first, me or mother?

And the courting went at a rapid pace:

Jack and Margaret at about the time of their marriage in 1937.

I always had a dog – everywhere I went I had a dog. I used to tie it up to the church gate while I was in church on Sundays. I had an old mac on, and a piece of string on the dog. That's how mother fell in love with me! We used to go a-courting down at Reymerston River. That's how we sort of – snowballed. I used to buy her a twopenny bar of Cadbury's milk chocolate – oh weren't that something! We went walking in Reymerston woods and her hands got cold so she put them in my pockets to warm. Well there was no bottom in them pockets! Whether that was a crafty move from me or not, it *was* as far as mother was concerned!

Then there was poor Helen – she was a big tall girl. Her and mother were

MY LIFE WITH HORSES

mates for quite a while up there. Mother used to have to wait at the table at eight o'clock at the hall – you'd hear the hand-bell all over the village, to call the Captain for supper. And 'cos mother was head maid and had to wait at table and Helen used to have to do all the clearing up, I used to look after Helen while mother was doing the necessary in the Hall.

And one evening Jack planned an 'overnight stay'!

As you go round the Hall, up the mile road especially, there's a big glass green-house on the corner of the hall and above that was the maids' bedroom. I kidded poor old mother and father up that I wouldn't be home that night. I was supposed to go to Bawdeswell 'cos mother's father was a keen draughts player and they had competitions in them days. I told them he had got a match on and a function. Well I chucked my old bike into that plantation and I nipped indoors time they were doing the necessary with the evening meal. I nipped up into the bedroom and laid underneath the bed. When old Mrs Hare (she was a parson's daughter) came to check the girls were in bed, I was laying underneath the bed and – well, we had some fun that night! The next morning I crept out of that window, slid down the board and got on my bike and went home.

There was no stopping Jack in them days. Two old policemen used to meet in the Hall corner – policemen always had their boundaries and they would always meet somewhere – that was a ritual then. Blast old Captain Hare, he had four Alsatian dogs chained up with big old chains. It was a long way up that drive. Captain Hare reckoned there was a bull out and he was chasing this bull up the drive – but of course it was me weren't it! He pulled up against those policemen and said, 'Bull out, bull out, have you seen a bull?' That was a laugh in the village then, 'Have you seen the bull?'

That was while mother was working there that I crept up to the kitchen window one day and made mother jump, and she dropped and broke some best china! Another time I remember Captain Hare's favourite old black cat Meffie. Well, the girls used to serve the evening meal and while this was being cleared up they used to sit and have their food. Nearly always as they were eating, the dirty old cat used to do its business. So I was there one night and it went to do that and I told them to catch the cat. They caught it and I proceeded to put a drop of mustard underneath its tail. Well the old cat went to the door and after a minute or two it squawked and went straight out of the door and up the fir tree where he remained for a couple of days – and the old Captain was going round saying, 'Have you seen Meffie?'

When Margaret found another job it meant a lot of added cycling for Jack:

When mother left there she went and got a job in Norwich, down on the Yarmouth Road at the Lansdown Hotel. It's 14 mile from Reymerston, it's 14 mile from the hotel to Bawdeswell and it's 14 mile from Bawdeswell home to Reymerston. I'd go up there every fortnight on a Sunday afternoon to meet mother at two o'clock and escort her to Bawdeswell. When you got to Swanton Morley with the church on the corner, there's a hell of a hill down there. I used to pedal like hell down there to get in front of her so I could see her skirt blow up 'cos in those days you weren't allowed to see knees! She'd be trying to hold her skirt down and I could see right up her leg. You can see when the mini-skirt came into fashion how that hit our generation!

I had to leave her in Bawdeswell and come back to Reymerston to milk those two or three old cows for Stanley Mortlock, then I'd bike back again to Bawdeswell and take her back to the Lansdown Hotel. I've come from the Lansdown Hotel at 10.30 at night, clean through Norwich – down Earlham Hill with no lights, 'cos we couldn't afford no batteries for lights. I used to freewheel down the hill. I used to have to get off 'cos two policemen always met on the bridge. I'd be a walking and pushing my bike over there and as soon as I got out of sight I got on and straight through Barford and onto Skipping Block Corner.

Wednesdays, once a fortnight, she went home alone, and I used to leave Reymerston to bike over there and take her back to the hotel.

Margaret became pregnant, and the couple were faced with marriage at a very young age:

I started a-courting mother and things happened, but you see I'm talking about 65 years ago. It was a terrible thing in those days to get a girl into trouble. Father, he washed his hands of it and you couldn't argue with him 'cos he was stone deaf. The only way was to shout – and then the whole village would hear. 'You've made your bed, you'll have to lie on it!' Well, that was left to my poor old mother!

Jack with the bike he had to sell to get married (late 1930s).

I bought a bicycle – a new Hercules bicycle – with no fancy work, no three-speed or nothing. Three pounds something and I'd got to pay three and sixpence a week. And if you kept the payments up you got the last week for nothing. I've got the card now where that was signed that I kept my payments up. Well I had to go and tell mother about Margaret and I was cleaning my bicycle up in the back kitchen and she say, 'What you going somewhere?'
'No,' I say, 'I've got to sell it – we've got to get married.'
That's when I told my mother. I'd got the bicycle upside down in the kitchen and that's when I broke the news. Well, there was arguing with my mother and sister Olive, but I stuck to my guns. It was my responsibility and I was going to get married. I've never regretted it. So we stayed with them until we went to Deopham.

It was a a stroke of good luck for Jack that Geoffrey Peacock came to farm in Reymerston, as it led to an important new job for the young lad, working for Geoffrey's father:

I used to ride the horses in the harvest field and Geoffrey Peacock took that little farm next door to us. The lands joined and we co-operated a lot. Sometimes I'd go and ride his horse. They used to put two on the binder or the pole 'cos you had to mow round the field so the horses didn't trample on the corn. You'd be swinging the scythe and the man behind would be tying up the bundles and putting them out of the way. They would put two horses on the pole to do the first round and then they had one tied to the gate. They put a contraption on the pole and there would be one on the outside and they would be three abreast. Some people had one on the front, but they always wanted a boy on the front horse to turn the corners. Geoffrey Peacock knew me and I were supposed to be a real good man on the farm! They all knew Jack was good for leading the horses. When he knew I was in trouble (when I got mother in the family way) and I was struggling, he told me that his father could do with a lad like me. I biked over and see the old man – that were old Lidlaw (William Lidlaw) Peacock. He was a tall old man and he used to wear a white stiff collar with a stiff front, and a white moustache. He was a hard man but also a hard-working man. He frightened me! You were frightened of your governor in them days, and if they said jump you jumped! You had got a job so you'd got something.

And young Jack, now with family responsibilities – husband and dad – could not look a gift-horse in the mouth:

Well when I was a-bargaining with him on the doorstep, I was shaking. I was terrified. And he bargained with me and his last words were, 'Oh you're living with your parents?' He say, 'Why don't you try this for a week or two and see how you like being here?' Seven mile that was – crafty old bugger. He was going to try me out! On the 7 January. I biked over there on mother's old bike. I got there at seven o'clock and I put an old strawberry roan mare in a big old iron-wheeled wagon. I drove that back to Reymerston and we put the bed on and bits and pieces somebody had found us. A couple of chairs somebody else had found us and we packed them on there. We put the pram on and we went back to Deopham – and that was when I moved into that little cottage. When I got there the only thing we ever bought brand-new was an oak gate-legged table.

William Lidlaw Peacock (c. 1940s) the first of four generations of the Peacock family that Jack worked for.

The cottage at High Tree Corner, Deopham (late 1930s).

Sparsely furnished the little cottage may have been, but it was a home of their own for the young parents. Margaret recalls how they had one candle to last them the week. This would be 'nipped out' as soon as possible, once the blazing wood fire had illuminated the room. The wood collected in an old pram was of course free, and helped to eke out the limited amount of coal they could afford each week:

It was a stick and coal fire and candle light. Bryan, he was born at North Green and father was worried about him. He used to say, 'That gal's milk en't no good for him.' He started giving him a little bread and sop – which was when mother used to cube up dried bread and pour boiling water over it, then drain off the water and put in some butter and salt and pepper. Father used to sit with this baby on his lap 'cos he was only little, and he put a little of this sop on a spoon. That's what father used to do twice a day for weeks! Then when we put him to

bed, you had a boiled sweet tied up in a bit of rag and pinned it on his chest and he used to lay and suck it – but he couldn't swallow it, could he? That was a regular thing that was, then.

In connection with this 'bread and sop' Margaret remembers cutting off about three inches from each end of a loaf of bread and scooping the centre out to make bread and sop for breakfast. She would then put a piece of cheese and an onion into the crust to make a good hearty lunch – with a bottle of tea.

There were plenty out of work, so Jack had to learn to do the job and be grateful – and try to keep out of trouble.

On a Friday night, I've stood in that yard waiting to get my orders and I've seen three good men walking around the corner not a rag to their back – three good honest working-men, hoping the governor was going to beckon them in for something special. I knew what I was going to get Friday night if I worked and kept my mouth shut. My first Friday night I took home 27/6d.

Old man Lidlaw, I can hear him now. He used to sit in that room and there was 11 of us going up to the door. I being the youngest, was on the end of the queue. When I got to the door I would say, 'There is a dozen rats' tails,' and he'd say, 'Alright Myrtle, give the boy the money,' and he come out of the door and he say, 'I think I had better take charge of them, boy, I think they may have come up last week!' But anyway I got my shilling.

The men working for Mr Peacock Senior had an early warning system of his approach:

We'd all be in a gang knocking these beet up. There'd be five or six of us pulling the beet, knocking them and laying them in rows. When the mould come off then they would come along and take the tops off the sugar beet and we'd be a-talking. All of a sudden the governor come across. The little old white spotted dog, a little old terrier, she used to be a god-send to us. The governor used to walk across the whole farm. He used to have gaps in the hedges where he'd come across. But Tiny, she'd allus come through the hedge first and she'd be a-barking, 'Look out, Look out!' The old man could see you, so you wouldn't be talking too much then. While he was about you'd keep going. I'm talking about 1940, not 1840!

He'd come through the field where we were carting sugar-beet. As we were filling our carts, he would come strolling in there with his little old dog. He'd say, 'I had a letter from the factory this morning, wanted to know if I had sold all my cows'. Then off he'd go. He meant, we were leaving too many leaves on the sugar-beet!

I can remember when Gents (?) they moved in a bloke. He come there as cowman from Lincolnshire. He'd mix up a big heap of chaff and mangolds and things and then he'd load it into skips and feed the cattle and then he'd go home and have his breakfast. Well he was coming back one morning and Lidlaw met him in the yard – he hadn't been there above two days. The old man he say, 'What yer had yer breakfast old partner? Where did you have it, in the bloody hearth?' And off he went. And the cowman say, 'Whatever did he mean?' Well, what he meant was, he had trod through the animals' food, jamming it into the ground, because he was in a hurry to get it off the heap. He hadn't bothered to stop and sweep it up.

If you did have a chat when you should have been working, you made sure there was no evidence:

I've had horses on a plough and mother or somebody would come past and you'd shout over the hedge and have a word with them. When you turned round to go back to your plough you would scuffle the ground where you'd been, so if the governor came through the hedge, he shouldn't see where you'd been standing.

Young Jack was keen to make a good impression on his new boss, and he explains how he did so in an interesting letter that survives. It was written from 'High Tree Corner, to his sister Hilda, in his first few months at Deopham, and gives us an insight into the young man, and just how hard he was working:

Dear Hilda, I hope you won't be too ill after this terrible shock, but it has played on my mind so long that I can't bear it any longer, so as you see I am writing at last to thank you very much for my birthday present which I was very pleased with. So sorry to keep you so long waiting to hear from me, but I really have been very busy. Wegg has left, so I have been team-man for a month till another man come, and have been up and into the stables every morning before five o'clock, till seven. Twenty minutes for breakfast and then tractoring till six and seven at night and then feeding the horses by lamp light after tea. Both the old man and the two sons, G. and P. all told me I improved the horses greatly after the first few days. You can bet I did too. I spent a good many hours combing and brushing them, I can tell you, and I used to think something of myself when I was using them, as I was head-man then, and the second horseman was the man that has been here 40 years. I had the two best horses in the stable, which nobody only the head-man is allowed to use, so I have been knocking up about 35/- a week now.

Bryan is doing fine now. M. takes him to a kind of clinic for babies in Hingham once a month, and last month she took him he weighed nine pounds and this month he weighed 12½ lbs, so he has gained nearly a lb a week. And I have had my orders to tell you that he has 5 Ovaltine rusks in the morning, a cup full of sop at night and as much cow's milk as what six cows can give, so he ought to be alright.

Well now I must close although I have tons more to write about, but I would like to get to bed as I am very tired, got the backache, headache, heartburn and altogether B… rotten.
Cheerio, lots of love,
Bryan, Mag and Jack.

Jack was to suffer from 'heartburn' all his life, but often claimed to be the real inventor of 'Rennies'! He remembers getting a piece of chalk out of a clay lump wall with his knife, and sucking that all day. Doctors were not troubled needlessly, so improvised cures had to be found.

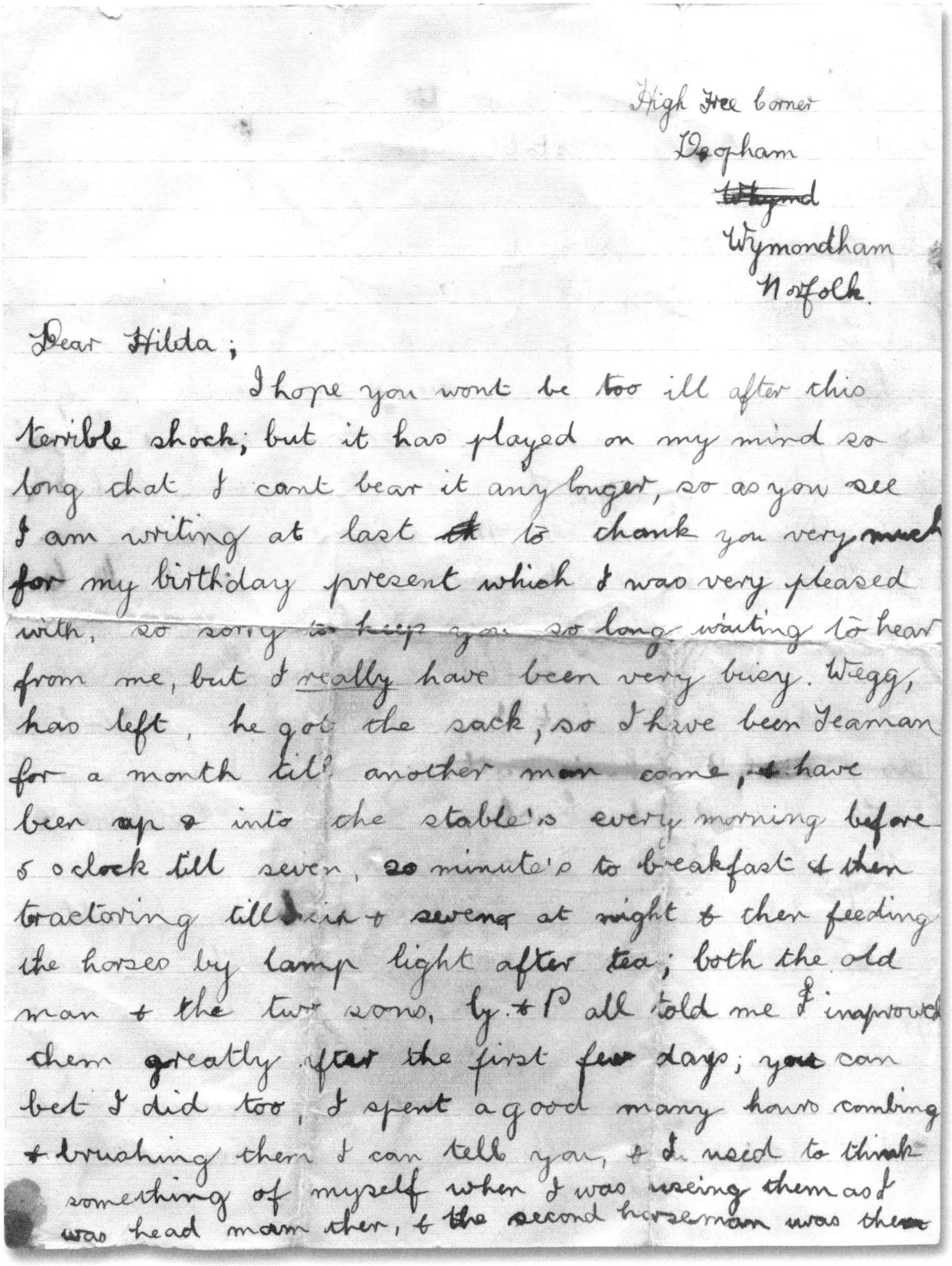

High Tree Corner

Deopham

~~Hingend~~

Wymondham

Norfolk.

Dear Hilda;

I hope you wont be too ill after this
terrible shock; but it has played on my mind so
long that I cant bear it any longer, so as you see
I am writing at last to thank you very much
for my birthday present which I was very pleased
with, so sorry to keep you so long waiting to hear
from me, but I really have been very busy. Wegg,
has left, he got the sack; so I have been Teaman
for a month till another man come, I have
been up & into the stable's every morning before
5 oclock till seven, 20 minute's to breakfast & then
tractoring till six & seven at night & then feeding
the horses by lamp light after tea; both the old
man & the two sons, Ly & P all told me I improved
them greatly after the first few days; you can
bet I did too, I spent a good many hours combing
& brushing them I can tell you, & I used to think
something of myself when I was useing them as I
was head man there, & the second horseman was there

Letter written to Hilda shortly after Jack and Margaret were married. (Final page of letter overleaf)

man that has been here 40 years, & I had the 2 best horses in the stable which nobody only the headman is allowed to use, so I have been knocking up about 35/- a week now.

Bryan is doing fine, M takes him to a kind of clinic at Hingham for babies once a month & last month she took him he weighd 9 lbs & this month he weighed 12½ lbs, so he has gained nearly 1 lb a week & I have had my orders to tell you that he has 5 Ovaltine rusks in the Morning, a cup full of sop at night, & as much cows milk as what 6 cows can give so he ought to be alright.

Well now I must close although I have tons more to write about, but I would like to get to bed (as I am old like to get to bed) as I am very tired, got the backache, headache, heartburn, & altogether B——— rotten.

Daddy has been over with on the old m & ther they went on to Ixworth. I'v mostly go over one night a week & they after come over to see me & Bobby is crazy to get over here, & has had 2 or 3 weekends here & he always want to stop longer. I will write again soon, so Cheerio lots of love & x x x x x x x
Bryan. Mag: & Jack

Final page of letter written to Hilda shortly after Jack and Margaret were married.

One of the jobs Jack liked at this period of his life, and one he was good at – was milking:

When I got to Deopham, there I could milk 22 cows morning and night for the old man, (Lidlaw Peacock) by hand. He used to come up to the house and he'd have big old aluminium pails and you'd have your milking pail. He'd come with the aluminium pail and you used to have to empty your pail into the aluminium one. He'd come down and take two pail-fulls up to the house and put them over a freezer. There was a recess at the top and that used to hold a pail-full of milk. That used to come down and go over the top of water. This cold water used to run over top of like a radiator thing – that's how they used to cool it and that would go into 17-gallon churns that come up to a narrow neck and the top thick old lid. In the middle of the lid was a hand-hold, and you'd put your hand onto that and you could roll that up the yard easy as anything. They used to have to go onto the wooden stand on the side of the road where a lorry could pull up. They had to be there by eight o'clock in the morning. I've sat and milked 22 head of cows one after the other. Stick your old head into her flank and you're away. There's something nice about it. Girls would come from different houses after the milk, in the morning. I sometimes used to get the old teat and spray it their way! One or two of the old cows would kick or sometimes they put their foot into the pail – oh all sorts of things.

For the young couple, things were extremely tight financially:

The original stove bought for 3/6d from Turners of Hingham in the late 1930s.

I used to have to go for two hours on a Sunday morning to help the old man move these sheep, and that paid for the rent. We bought a little old stove from Charles Turner in Hingham – an established firm who used to come round by horse and cart (later-on he had a van). He'd always come through Wicklewood and then to Deopham. He came through Deopham at six o'clock on a Saturday night. He used to sell all sorts: bootlaces, boot polish, haberdashery, paraffin and that sort of thing. We decided to get this little stove with one wick in it – three and sixpence it was. I think mother paid eighteen pence for it, and then we paid sixpence a week. Well that got to the third week and we hadn't got the sixpence! So we put the fire out, we put the candle out and we put the bar over the back door, and we hid up like a couple of little frightened mice! He banged and banged at that old door! He went round to next door and I reckon he asked, 'What are they out next door?' They said, 'They were there a little while ago!' He came back and rattled and banged at the door and we sat there and we daren't breathe! There we were married, and got a child and I was getting a man's wage and we were frightened! We heard his old van go down the road round those 's' bends, and we watched his lights go past the old man's farm and we knew he weren't coming back again after his sixpence.

From that day mother never owed anybody a penny. Even when she worked down at the shop all those years for Mrs Ruthven at Morley, if she wanted some stuff and she hadn't got enough on her, she would go home and get her purse then come back to collect the stuff. She was working there but she never wanted to owe anybody.

Margaret developed tuberculosis and their son Bryan also had a septic knee. A neighbour, Mrs Downes, had a little girl the same age, and the two wives became friends. When a visit to Norwich hospital was necessary, Mrs Downes accompanied Margaret.

I got a pair of horses on the six-acre field near Deopham School and I was plough-ing up old sugar-beet land, ready for barley the next year. Water laid everywhere. I'd got my old boots on but my feet were sodden. I was trying to keep my feet warm but the water kept coming into the furrow as I went up and as I come back. As I turned, who should come up the road but the two women with their little prams. Just past the school you can come down there to Deopham church and go down to Kimberley Station, but mother avoided that 'cos if they walked to Wymondham, it was a penny-ha' penny cheaper to get the train to go to Norwich. I had a chat with the little old boy and said cheerio and they went off up the road. Mother was walking on the side of her foot. She'd been trying to patch her shoes up 'cos they'd got holes in. She'd got an old bit of leather off my old boots and the bloody nails had come through! She was hobbling off to Wymondham to save a penny-ha'penny on the train. I don't mind admitting, I cried. I thought, 'what have we done to deserve this?'

It was a hard life trying to make ends meet in those early days, with no real safety net in the form of a 'dole', although 'parish relief' was available for some:

I was in work but there weren't no dole then. The first dole house that opened up was Attleborough – that would be about the beginning of the wartime. There would be people like Captain Hare, the parson, people in big houses and the big farms who would come by with baskets with something left over – half a loaf of bread, or half a pie or something.

As you go from where I lived at Deopham towards Hingham there're sharp 's' bends, and there is a big grass verge with a hedge. Two or three men would bike there for half past six in the morning and stop there all day with their barrows and things working on the little hedges to make them better looking. They are there now, those hedges. They used to get six bob if they went for two or three days. That was parish relief. Wintertime, when we got snowed up – 'cos we used to then – they used to have to clear the snow and dig paths out, clearing anywhere that was snowbound. They'd get extra for that – otherwise it was bloody hard. They were hard times and it makes me sick nowadays, these young chaps of 45 and 50, they ridicule them and say 'I would have told them to get stuffed.' I heard of that enough on the farm, and I used to say, 'No you would-n't, if you'd got a wife and child, and a decent wage coming in, you'd keep your mouth shut.' They just cannot take that in. It grieves me sometimes to hear. You see you can stand up now and argue with your employer – in fact he hardly dares argue with you! It's got out of hand.

Jack was always looking for that extra job – and a little more money:

It was getting towards Christmas and I was getting a bit desperate then. You wanted a bit extra for Christmas. Then old man Peacock he say to me, 'If you want to earn a little extra for Christmas you can go and mould up the two heaps of mangolds on that six acre.' Well, you see, that was on the six acres on the bottom field at Deopham. They used to cart the mangolds and heap them up, but because mangolds are full of water, if you got a frost on them they wouldn't be any good. So you used to have to straw them and then dig a trench round the bottom of the heap and then you'd put a foot of mould on. He found me a hurricane lantern! You'd dig a trench – about a yard wide – and I've known him to walk through there and he'd put a stick in where I had patted the mould to see that I hadn't put a thin layer on.

Then three weeks afore Christmas you'd go a-plucking. Clarkes (?) in the village they had turkeys, and I used to sit there until two o' clock in the morning plucking turkeys. You used to have a ladder and you'd tie them up. Then they would pick them up at five o'clock the next morning and they'd go off to where they sold them. Fifteen shilling I earnt one Christmas. Then one year Cecil Matheson (?) – he was in poultry – he made a bargain. When I went home to tea at night there would be two or three crates of chickens standing by the old shed ready for me to pluck and truss. I could pluck them at home and then he'd pick them up at four or five o'clock in the morning and take them off to the station. That saved me running about. Then always, whatever I earned extra above my wages, I'd go 50/50 with mother.

Another job that Jack helped with was threshing, vastly different from using today's combines:

The first Spring I was there old Bob Flint he used he do almost a week's thrashing in four or five days, he'd do it in. They were little farms then and that was my job to cart the corn. I had the stallion what you couldn't work with! Anything else I had to have in a single cart to cart the water to the wheat stack. The old engine would take three load of water – old iron-wheeled water carts – you'd take them down into the pit. You'd stand down on a step in the pit and load them and pull that up to the engine to keep Bob's steam up. You'd take a quarter of a ton of steam coal and all the corn sacks and the chaff sacks. That would be your first job in the morning to get them up, then come home and get a load of water. Then put the horse back into the tumbril and cart seven or eight load of sacks of corn on the tumbril. You'd take them back to the barn – carry them into the barn and go back again – and there would be another load ready for you!

You'd do about three loads and then Bob he'd be whistling on, 'I want some more water.' You'd have to drop your tumbril off and put your horse into the water cart down into the pit to get another load of water. I used to carry 18 stone of corn off the back of the cart into the barn and set it up high against the wall – big old sacks. Them old corn sacks when they tied them up they had a bit to spare out of the top and you'd pull it over so when you set the other one on that would be set up straight and tidy. Eighteen stone of wheat, 16 stone of barley, 12 stone of oats, 24 for linseed. I've gone home at night and I've cried when mother has peeled my shirt off my back. I had to go back the next day, and I can feel it now, getting up against that first bloody sack and I'd hardly dare put it onto my shoulders. My skin was raw – I've cried. Calamine lotion – weren't that lovely to feel over your back? You knew you'd got to go the next day and I wouldn't give in. It was only my headstrong determination kept me going. Times were hard – do you know we used to sit back to back to eat our dinner – that way we rested our backs. You had to, it was bloody hard work in them days. Years later, before combines, there were baggers. They bagged and you'd drive round and put them on the field and then two or three would come and lift them up and take them home.

Even though people in the villages were so hard up, camaraderie was still an important factor. For example Jack remembered that meals were frequently communal affairs. One group of wives might be responsible for delivering the dinners, which everyone shared, and the second group would do likewise for the 'fourses', mid-afternoon.

It was while he was with Mr Peacock that Jack obtained his first driving licence:

I got my first driving licence in 1937, which was when I was at Peacocks at Deopham in that little old cottage. I had the first tractor around there – an old Fordson with no mudguards, and spiked wheels. It had a double-furrow plough, on wheels. There was a four-acre field opposite Deopham 'Half Moon', down at Pettengills Farm. I've been in there with the tractor and plough, working for different farmers. Mr Dring with his pony and cart and Mr Bales on his bike watching me plough up and down in that field.

Jack on an early tractor, believed to be on Peacock's farm at Deopham.

And the early tractors could be decidedly difficult to work with:

In them days the tractor had those heavy old iron wheels and then that bloody track rod would snap. It was nobody's fault but it would snap! Well then I had to get on my bike and go into Attleborough with these two bits and get old Gerry Reeves the blacksmith to weld them. Of course there wasn't no such thing as welding as we know it now, but he used to get these two bits and they'd measure them and get the chalk mark on them. They'd get the two ends white hot, two of them, and they would hammer them together. That old track rod got full of knots and bumps but they had to get it as right as they could. It was always breaking because of the vibration from the tractor with the heavy old wheels – I'm talking of 60 year ago.

On one occasion a visit to the blacksmith meant a bit of subterfuge:

One Monday at the back of the farm near the school, the track rod snapped and I had to take that to Attleborough. Well Myrtle, (Lidlaw's daughter) she'd got a car, big old square type brown Austin – that was in the garage round the back of the farm. It was Monday, washday, and the old man he say,
'I daren't ask her to go as it's washday. Jack, what are we going to do?'
'Well,' I say, 'I shall have to bike in with it.'
He say, 'You can drive a tractor – can't you drive that old motor?'

So we crept round there and undone those doors right quietly and we pushed that motor down onto the road towards the shop, so Myrtle couldn't hear us. We started it up and off I went to Gerry Reeves. Weren't I King of the Castle – weren't I somebody! I drove into his little old drive and messed about waiting for it to be done. Well, Percy (Myrtle's brother) had his farm just up the road, and he'd come into Attleborough for something, only to see the car stand there! So he come to see what was going on. He say,'Where's Myrtle?'

There was a hell of a do then! Myrtle had to bike in and put her bike in the back and take it home again. I hadn't got a licence, had I? Three or four days later a little red cardboard thing come through the post – that was my driving licence! I never had to take my test. I got what they called a 'grandfather's licence'. All you had to do was sign a paper to say you'd been driving that type of vehicle so long and you were quite capable, and that was enough.

A Young Stallion Man

Despite his problems financially, as far as Jack was concerned, his life was opening out. It was at Deopham that he began his career as a stallion man. Jack's initiation into 'stallion walking', whilst working for Peacocks, came about in a strange way – through a boisterous horse:

I was working on the farm, driving the first tractor that had been in the district for miles – a little Fordson. During the week Percy (Peacock) came to the Deopham farm in his little old Morris. He come tearing after me, 'I got another job for you,' he say. 'I got to take you to Barnham Broom 'Bell' to collect a horse. Old Bailey (publican of the Horningtoft 'Hurdle') has had a lot of trouble with the horse.' He'd broke out and smashed up some bicycles at the pub and one thing and another. He'd been naughty and Old Bailey wouldn't have him, so he'd brought him back to Barnham Broom 'Bell'. Percy took me over there to pick up the pony and cart and the stallion, and bring him back to Deopham.

Well the next day or two there was ructions with old man Lidlaw and the two sons. What were they going to do about all those mares booked out and nobody to see to them? So old Charlie Skipper, a professional leader, come home the week-end with his horse Flash Boy and he was sleeping with us those two nights. He got onto old Lidlaw and he say, 'You send that boy off, he'll be alright – you send him off on Monday morning.'

Margaret remembers watching from the bedroom window, somewhat sadly, as Jack went off at the beginning of the week with his pony and trap, and his stallion.

So off I went Monday morning with the pony and cart loaded up with my grub, and chaff and corn for the horse underneath, and the little old dog beside me. I called at Burt's Farm first, then Hardingham Hall Farm. Old Mr Harrold he had a little old terrier dog there. It kept biting your heels while we stood there talking – little bastard! Then away from there into Hardingham, two or three farms in Hardingham, then finished up in Reymerston and Geoffrey's farm. I stayed at North Green Monday night and then in the morning went up to Emma Stanford's farm and Beckett's farm – two mares there – and so on. I got half way up Reymerston Mile Road and I realized I hadn't got a penny in my pocket. I was hoping to see my Dad working up there and hoping I could borrow a pound, when Geoffrey Peacock come up the road in his little old motor. He'd forgot to send me off with any money!

Jack on one of the first tractors.

'The Stallion Leader', a painting by Joe Godderidge. This was a painting based on Jack, with his pony and cart. The stallion was Pettengills Grey King.

Jack had a natural talent with horses and was soon making his way. It was true that stallion walkers had a certain reputation at the time – and of course there was always someone ready to plant a few seeds of doubt where a wife was concerned!

I used to be away all week and mother she'd go and stay a night at North Green (with my mother and father) and then perhaps the next day she'd go to Bawdeswell to see her people and have a night with them. I didn't come home until the Friday night, or perhaps the Saturday morning, and go off again the Monday morning. Anyway, that was the second year when she went over to my mother's for a couple of days and she went down to the village shop. The lengthman (like my father) knew everybody and as she was coming out of the shop he says,
'What you keep coming home for like this?'
'Well,' she says, 'my husband is away all week, so I'm on my own.' She let it out that I travelled the stallion around that way you see, and stayed out at nights.
'Oh,' he say, (that old bugger, he done it on purpose) 'I know him – I know who you're a-talking about. He come this way. He done that way last year and they reckon he left more foals than what the stallion did!' That got a laugh for years after. The stallion leaders were notorious for it, and they got a bad name for that.

But despite this reputation, it was a way of earning a reasonable wage, even if occasionally it required some effort to collect the fees.

Well, you see, I got extra money – three shillings 'groom fee' off the farmers – and if you had six mares along this farmer, you got three guineas for the stallion covering each mare and three shillings as my groom fee. I had to pay my lodgings but we got double a man's wages (which was 30 shillings a week), so we got three pound a week for 10 to 12 weeks, or whatever we bargained for with different farmers. Farmers were hard up then and I got wrong once for taking a post-dated cheque and that couldn't be paid for the next couple of months – but they *were* hard up. They most probably couldn't pay until they had sold the corn or something. One or two places I could get the post-dated cheque but I couldn't get my 15 shillings in cash. I used to have to bike there later on in the summer time, on a Sunday. There was one man over at Wood Dalling, I had to bike over there one or two times, but I *did* get my money.

Stallion walking in those early days was a competitive and highly organised operation, with printed cards giving details of each itinerary. Money could be made by those who had an aptitude:

On Dereham market place on a Friday there would be seven of us the first week of the season, the horses all braided-up and plaited-up, and with a pocket-full of cards with details of the name of the stallion and where you were going to stop at certain nights. The farmers would look round them – you'd walk them up and down. Then we used to go into the 'Bull' and feed the horse, and in the afternoon you'd go up and down again.

On one overnight stay at the 'Bull', it was necessary to walk the stallion onto the pavement to avoid the traffic. Unfortunately the horse caught sight of his reflection in the plate-glass window, and hit out with his fore-foot, smashing the window. Jack kept on walking!

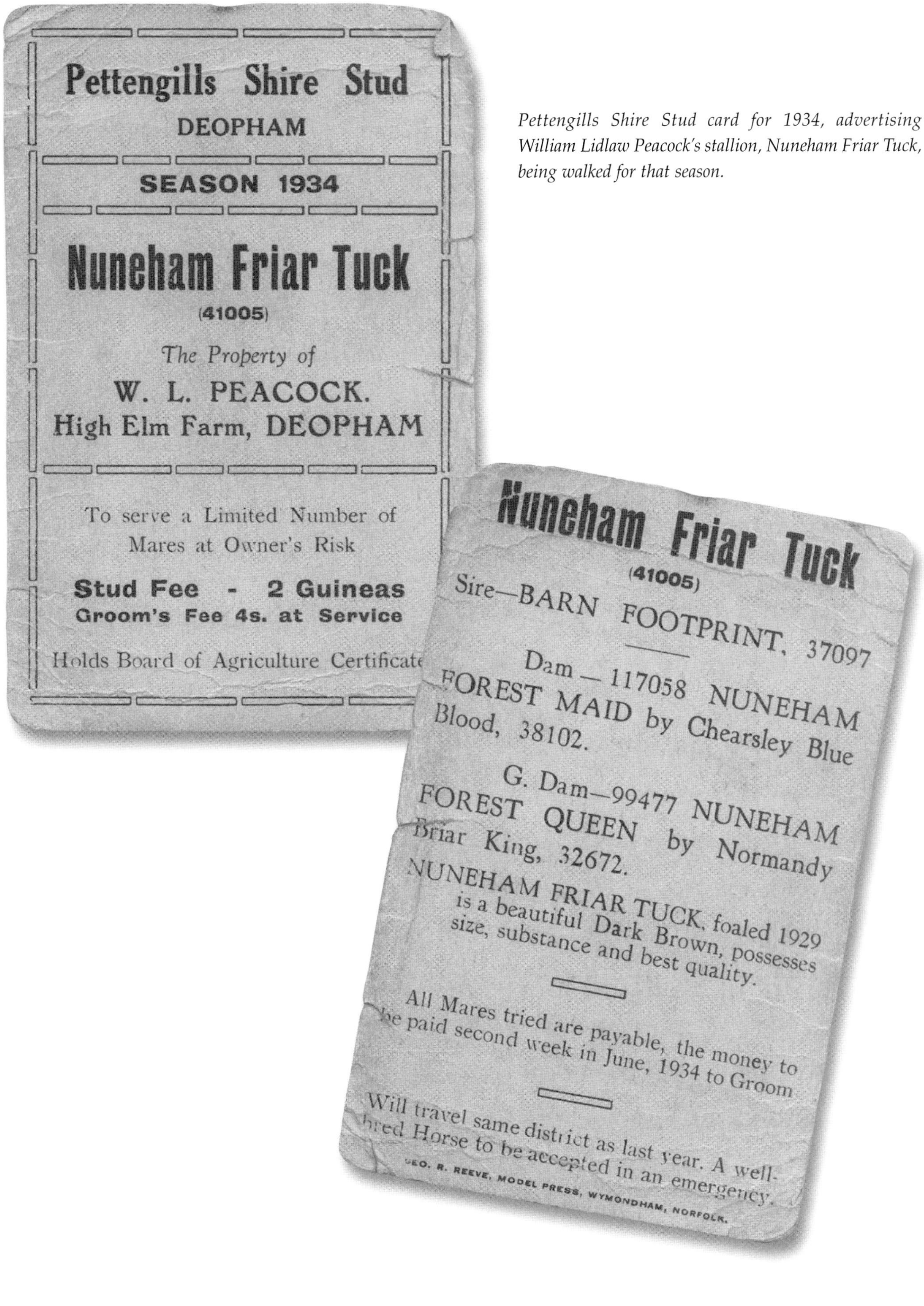

Pettengills Shire Stud

DEOPHAM

SEASON 1934

Nuneham Friar Tuck

(41005)

The Property of

W. L. PEACOCK.

High Elm Farm, DEOPHAM

To serve a Limited Number of
Mares at Owner's Risk

Stud Fee - 2 Guineas
Groom's Fee 4s. at Service

Holds Board of Agriculture Certificate

Nuneham Friar Tuck

(41005)

Sire—BARN FOOTPRINT, 37097

Dam — 117058 NUNEHAM
FOREST MAID by Chearsley Blue
Blood, 38102.

G. Dam—99477 NUNEHAM
FOREST QUEEN by Normandy
Briar King, 32672.

NUNEHAM FRIAR TUCK, foaled 1929
is a beautiful Dark Brown, possesses
size, substance and best quality.

All Mares tried are payable, the money to
be paid second week in June, 1934 to Groom

Will travel same district as last year. A well-
bred Horse to be accepted in an emergency.

GEO. R. REEVE, MODEL PRESS, WYMONDHAM, NORFOLK.

Pettengills Shire Stud card for 1934, advertising William Lidlaw Peacock's stallion, Nuneham Friar Tuck, being walked for that season.

Stallion walking during the war period was of course more difficult with all the signposts removed in case of invasion. Even names on farm carts were taken off. During this time Jack remembered being unable to get accommodation in a pub near an American air-base – or rather, the horse was accommodated but not Jack. So he turned the cart upside down near the stable, and Jack and his little dog slept under it. During the night however, there was a terrible air-raid:

A terrifying experience – each bomb seemed nearer, and the last one set the walls vibrating and started the cart wheels revolving, which they continued to do for an incredibly long time. The horse snorted a bit but it was surprising how he accepted the situation.

The process of stallion walking was regulated by the heavy horse societies, and Jack describes the way the societies worked:

The different societies, different breeds, used to travel their stallions round the country. The Norfolk branch of the Suffolk Horse Society had 12 stallions one year travelling the county of Norfolk. Walker from Norwich, he had about 10 out – all stallions hired by the Society, to travel where they told you to travel. They were responsible and they took the money, and if you didn't make a profit that was their fault, that weren't the farmers'. The farmers were on a good thing. They knew what they were going to get and it was up to the grooms to do the canvassing and get all the work, 'cos he was getting three shillings a mare.

With the Royal Family's interest in horses it is not surprising that Jack met several members over the years. Jack remembers talking to Prince Charles about his stallion-walking days, six decades before, and his own association with Sandringham. For a time Jack walked a horse called Sandringham Scapa (7084), originally bred by King George VI, and subsequently owned by A.A.Walker of East Dereham.

That was what I was talking to Prince Charles about. He said, 'You stayed in pubs, you say – in pubs every night?'.
'Yes,' I say, 'and three shillings didn't go very far, I can tell yer!'
'I suppose that didn't. What was the object of travelling?' he asked.
'Well I had to go to tend to the mares.'
'Oh yes, of course, I understand.'
I said to him, 'As a matter of fact, on a Thursday I used to come through the middle of the Sandringham Estate, and occasionally I was called in to attend to one of their mares.'
'Really,' he said, 'and why was that?'
'Because their resident stallion, their own, was probably related to her. In them days,' I said, 'I beg your pardon but I'm talking of 60 to 65 year ago, Sandringham was the biggest and most noted stud of Suffolk horses in this country.'
'Really?'
'Oh yes,' I said, 'it was a pleasure to see them at work on all them fields. As a matter of fact,' I said, 'I once travelled a stallion called Sandringham Scapa.'

I also remember talking to Princess Anne who asked what I was doing with a Suffolk stallion when she had previously seen me with a Percheron.
'No colour bar here Ma'am!' I replied.

Windsor Park, in front of the Queen. Jack Juby is second from the left.

Being presented to the Queen: The Queen commented, 'My word, isn't he alert.'

Talking to Prince Philip.

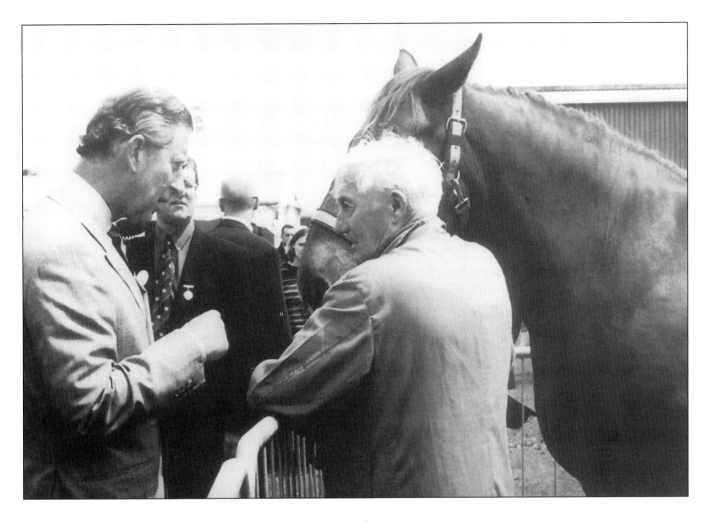

Above: *Talking to Prince Charles: Jack tells him how he used to visit the Sandringham Estate. The horse was Peggy Sue of Withersfield.*

Right: *Meeting the Duke of Kent.*

Although the stallion leaders were itinerant professionals, unattached to individual farms, there were young men like Jack, with an aptitude for the job, working in the same way, but as wage earners for a particular farmer.

I was working for Peacocks in the first place – that's where I had my introduction. I had to take a two year old – Pettengills Grey King – from Deopham. He was supposed to belong to Percy. One belonged to Percy , one belonged to Geoffrey and one belonged to the old man. Three of us used to go off Monday morning different ways. Charlie Skipper with Flash Boy, he done the Watton area, 'Old Sugar' he done the Forncett area and all out that way, and I did Dereham and Fakenham with Pettengills Grey King. I done that first circuit because I had been looking after the stallions for weeks and weeks afore, feeding them and getting them ready for these stallion leaders. Stallion leaders in them days were professional men – they didn't work on the farm. Old Quadling (?) from Lowestoft, he'd come to Peacock's year in and year out to travel his stallion in that district, and then when the season was over they were gone. Old Bob Bailey, he kept Horningtoft 'Hurdle', the Pub there. He had one of Peacock's horses to do the Dereham and Fakenham district for the season.

Jack with the stallion Pettengills Grey King (c. late 1930s), one of the first stallions he walked. Note the cartwheel in the background. He needed a pony and cart to transport the horse feed for the week.

And the annual arrival of gypsies usually offered a little work, 'off the record':

Every year, about three or four times, there'd be these gypsies. They all had horses then – biggish cobs, and there'd be one or two you knew you were going to see. They'd be sleeping along the way and they'd got a mare and they'd want it serviced. You used to get a pound for that, and it didn't go in the books you see!

Jack greatly enjoyed his involvement with the horse sales:

There would be a sale in March every year and your governor, he'd send a couple of horses. Somebody would be there wanting a certain horse. They would be transported by lorry then. They had got contractors and the lorries were getting more numerous. Jock Reynolds had three cattle-floats on the road in them days. You'd take the horses to the sale and put them in the stalls and do their tails up. Different farmers would come along and they would be a-looking through the catalogue and they'd say, 'Well, wass he done, boy? Is he alright? Is he quiet? Has he been in the shafts?' Then you'd walk him up and down and they give you sixpence tip, you see.

It was on the way home from a sale one day that Jack first transported ice-cream:

Coming home from Ipswich sale one day, with Ray the regular driver, we pulled up at a café. There was a chap who runs this café – a regular stop for the lorry drivers. When we pulled up there to have a cup of tea we saw he had a freezer in the corner, the first one I ever saw! We drove all the way home with my hand out of the window to keep this block of ice cream cold! That'd be just afore the war.

Jack's remembered going to shows on Norwich Hill:

They had a stallion show every year at springtime and the Norfolk Society would get their stallions from the show. They hired 12 stallions one year, at the

Pineapple Hotel at Trowse! Anybody interested could come along on a Saturday and view the stallions. They'd ask what district you were doing, then you would make a bargain with them, how much and what time if you went there (say 11 o'clock on a Wednesday morning) and that would be your regular time then for the season. This was in the forties.

And Jack remembers that standards were not so high in those early days:

The first show I ever went to, to show horses, was at Beccles. I was about 16 or 17. I shew for Geoffrey Peacock – that was old Captain, a Percheron, in a single wagon. The things were not so up to date then. We had got a good set of harness then, but not like they are now. There weren't the number of classes and things. I remember Captain, he had got bad old feet, with great cracks, and we patched it all up with soap to fill in the cracks, and they looked alright time he was in the ring! But of course you don't get that today because different societies started getting classes for the best feet, and that improved people looking after the feet. 'Course some of it was caused through neglect and some through the breeding. That's why I used to cut the hoof down to get rid of the old. You can't grow a new hoof until you have got rid of the old. You see, they get a lot of pressure on the new bits if you haven't got rid of the old.

Accidents could easily happen, and were very frightening for young horsemen, especially in the show-ring:

Charlie Saunders had three different turn-outs there that day, and young Sid, who was driving one in the ring, was younger than I was. His father was head groom for Charlie Saunders. He got in a muddle and the horse 'jack-knifed', we called it. He pulled round too sharp and he turned the wagon over. That can happen as quick as lightning. I learned that, that day, and you never forget. I felt sorry for the boy because that really frightened him.

Jack explained the concept of 'upgrading' where horse breeding was concerned:

Geoffrey Peacock used to show Percherons but Lidlaw had Shires in the first place. Geoffrey, the son, he educated him that Shires were too hairy-legged and he crossbred them. You were allowed to do that with the Society. You could cover or serve this mare and get her in foal by a Percheron stallion and you could part-register the off-spring as a Percheron, or if that was a filly foal and that came of age, and you covered her with a full-bred Percheron, you could register *her* offspring as pure Percheron. 'Upgrading' they used to call that. When the inspectors come round they have a look at the animal to see if it was good enough to upgrade. So then it was that Geoffrey started off on the Percherons.

This life, working with horses, was all Jack ever wanted:

Working your horse was a natural thing. He was getting his exercise and being well fed and he was leaving a percentage of foals, the most natural thing. They were lovely times.

MOVING ON

Jack worked for Lidlaw Peacock for some time, and when the old man died, for various reasons he decided he needed a change. Joe Bales, a farmer in Deopham had a brother in Tittleshall, and suggested he might work for him. Unfortunately it did not work out, but luckily he had already been offered a place at Cranworth, working for a Mrs Wade, a job he took:

That was at Mrs Wade's at Church Farm Cranworth, that we used to have nosebags for the horses, big old bags that strapped over the head and half the bag was leather. While we were right up on the Watton road one day having our dinner, one of the old horses, an old mare, well, something must have bit the old mare and she took off and run home complete with tumbril! She run home and got into the pit and drowned herself! She went into the pit with her nosebag on and that filled with enough water so there was just enough in that leather piece and that drowned her.

But at this same time Letton Hall had an opportunity working with horses, and the temptation was too strong:

Then Harry Banham at Squire Gordon's was after me. I don't know why they always wanted me for horses, suppose 'cos I'd got that affinity, something anyway. They were all beautiful Suffolk horses then. I used to go down to the pub with Harry, and his sons Charlie and Sid. He actually took me away from Mrs Wade's to go to Blackmoor Row to Gurdon's Farm to a stud there, so I had another move right quick down there.

Letton Hall, Cranworth.

They had Suffolk horses there and I was noted for being a stallion man. Harry Banham was the steward on all them farms – Booton Farm, Home Farm, Gurdon's Farm, Cranworth Farm, Low Farm. They were all part of the big estate belonging to Squire Gordon of Letton Hall. There was a manager lived at Home Farm, a proper manager, and Harry Banham was 'bicycle riding steward'. They were all a nice family – Charlie, Sid and May. I always got on with Harry and he encouraged me to move to Letton Hall. So that's how I moved down to Blackmoor Row and I got breaking the horses in for the Hall.

They were all pure-bred Suffolk horses. There was a big picture in the *Dereham and Fakenham Times* when there were 27 Suffolk horses in one field from three farms all amalgamated. Tails were all done and their brasses on. They come and took a picture of the 27 horses!

But as well as earning money from his horse-breaking, Jack, the youngest worker, also learnt other useful skills:

I was the youngest one on the estate. As soon as you got to 21 your blue insurance stamp was more money. Up till then it was a green stamp and on all those farms I was the only one with a green stamp. I used to get a pound for every horse I broke in – if there was one 'wore up' on a certain farm, and they wanted a fresh one.

Harry Banham also got me into stacking, which was a full man's job, and shew me how to thatch. We used to get a pound for every stack we thatched (we got that at Christmas time) – that is if it didn't get on the lean too much. If so, when the water come down off the roof that would come down the edge of the stack and let the water in that side. 'On the piss' we used to call that! We used to get a pound for every one that was thatched without leaning.

Things were a little easier now financially, and they even had a wireless at that time:

Anyway that was all lovely then. We were getting a little extra money – a pound for this and a pound for that – and we were better off. In them days we had a wireless – they weren't radios that went with a battery, these went with those little old accumulators. I used to bike to Shipdham with it to Rudling's and get them to charge the accumulator up every little while.

And of course Jack remembered well the day his second son Kenny was born – and enlisting his mother again in her role as midwife:

Blackmoor Row, that was where Kenny was born. My poor old mother – midwife again! She biked from Reymerston up the mile road to look after Margaret – on the 10th March 1942. I can show you the field now. I come from the farm with my pair on a drill, at seven o'clock. Ten minutes past seven you was into the field. You'd go round the field twice with the drill, so when you started on the field you knew where to start and pick your drill up, and start your seed. Then when you got round to the headland you knew where to stop the drill so you didn't go over where you had started to drill. That was the marker. There was frost that night on the plantation and the sun hadn't got over there, so I done the two ends where I got to turn.

Ten o'clock that morning my mother come biking up the road on her old bicycle. She had got a bottle of hot tea wrapped up in old socks and things, to keep hot, and she say, 'you've got a curly-headed little boy.' I was in my shirt sleeves and the hosses were a sweating. For two days mother'd bike home, to see to things at home.

When it came to giving his mother a little something for all her help, the usual problem of lack of money came to the fore:

A few days later my mother said it was time for Margaret to look after herself. Then I say, 'What are we going to give mother?' Hadn't got a ha' penny! Anyhow all the labourers were allowed a brace of rabbits once a month, or something half price or whatever, and it was my turn. 'I know, I'll give mother a brace of rabbits.' I said to Sid (Banham) that morning, 'Can you get me a brace of rabbits?' Teatime that night mother was still there ready to pack up and go home. Margaret said, 'Here come Sid up the yard with a brace of rabbits.' He put his bike against the gate and he come up the path with his rabbits – proud as punch. But it was Thursday night and Friday was payday, weren't it! He wanted his half-crown to go down to Shipdham 'Standard' didn't he, and I hadn't got a bloody penny had I! So I went to the door, 'Cor blast Sid, I didn't expect to see you tonight. Have you got change for a pound?'

'No I hen't, John, you know that.'

I say, 'Never mind, I'll pay you tomorrow night.' Margaret, she say, 'However did you face him and say that!' Poor old Sid, he had to go without his pint that night!

Sadly Jack's time with the horses at Letton Hall came to an end when the estate was sold and Jack had the difficult job of preparing all his horses for the grand sale.

Jack skinning a rabbit in the 1940s.

Squire Gordon, sold up the whole of the estate. That was fatal, otherwise I'd have been there now – and of course all the horses had to go. Everything on the estate in them days had been worked with the horse. They had the biggest Suffolk horse sale round there for a long while, all down at Home Farm. And it was writ about in the paper that every horse had its tail done up, even the foals. They'd never seen foals' tails plaited up afore, and I took every one into the ring in front of the auctioneer. There was about 30 to 40 horses and I was up all night braiding and plaiting their tails up. That would be early 1940s.

Because that was a big sale, they came from all over the place to buy these pedigree Suffolk horses and one of the people who came was a Mr Holman from Aylsham. He'd got two farms, one at Marsham and one at Aylsham. Word got round – what's Jack going to do? He's a good stallion man. He's done up all their tails and shewed them. Well there was this chap from Acle and he came and had a word, and he say, 'That man there, Mr Holman, he's a good Suffolk horse and stallion man. I'll introduce you.' So he introduced me to Mr Holman and we made a bargain. I had to bike from Blackmoor Row on Sunday to Marsham. Twice I went up that tree-lined hill to find Grove Farm, and eventually I found it. I met the man, saw the house and made a bargain.

Sid Banham, later in life, at a darts match at Shipdham 'Standard' (c. late 1950s).

So the Juby family was on the move again, this time by courtesy of a coal lorry.

Pumphrey the coalman, he used to have two or three lorries and he used to work for Holman's, so it was bargained for him to come and pick us up from Blackmoor Row. We went through Dereham and called at the old secondhand furniture shop out on the Swanton Morley road that had been there for years. We called there and we bought a bureau.

Margaret remembers dyeing an old sheet pink to make curtains – one step up from the sacks they had to use at their windows at times. She also remembers distempering the walls to brighten them up.

And Jack was back with his beloved stallions again. Exercising these stallions confused his wife one day:

So when I got to Holman's, he had nine stallions. One day in particular I had to take each stallion out for exercise, you see. I used to walk them up that hill to Aylsham and back again. Well 'cos they were all Suffolk chestnuts, when I went into dinner mother couldn't make out what the hell I was doing going backwards and forwards. She thought I had got the same horse! That was when you used to have to exercise the stallions every day - when they were boxed up.

It was 1947, a very snowy year, at Marsham, when Margaret lost her mother. Jack was left with the two boys to look after, and was not very domesticated!

It was all snowed up and we had the two boys. We had tremendous snow all over the whole country. Charlie Skipper kept the pub at Marsham, 'The Plough'. He took mother over in a hurry to Bawdeswell. She was several days 'cos she couldn't get back no more and I was left with the two boys. That was when I made the dumplings and put them into cold water in the saucepan! After a little while I realized they should have been put into boiling water so I went to grab them out and they were sticking everywhere. The boys reckoned I was playing yo-yo with the dumplings to try and get them out of the saucepan again!

When poor mother come home, every dish in the house was all piled up in the sink. I hadn't done any washing-up nor nothing. I was never domesticated. The old hearth was full of cinder muck! I couldn't do it, you see. Kenny had to stop with the neighbours and Bryan went to school while I went to work. When mother came home she brought her younger sister Chris home to live with us, because she was still a girl.

Jack remembers at this time that his elder son needed financing – for his school 'wheeling and dealing'!

Bryan was at school and Kenny wasn't yet. One day Bryan came up past the big long cow house. He came up the lane that morning – I shall never forget, he weren't very old – tapping on the window so I would look through. He was off to school and he say:
'Can you lend me half a crown, boy?'(He always called me 'boy'.) He'd got a deal on with his boys up at the school. HALF A CROWN! There's me without a penny in my pocket.

When tractors became commonplace, the writing was on the wall for heavy horses, and the way of life on the farms that went with them. Jack was in at the very end of this chapter of agricultural life:

The stallions were getting less 'cos the tractors were getting about, that was when a lot of stallion people give up, you see. But Holman stuck it and we got a Ford lorry and put the stallion on. He took me round for two or three weeks and then he got me to drive certain places and then after that he got me to go round on my own. I used to do Dereham , Fakenham and a big farm out by Sculthorpe and all round Holkham and that way. Some of them wanted six mares serviced and they'd bring out eight you see, hoping that they'd get six of them in foal. They'd come out that morning and they'd say, 'I want old so and so this week'. Then they'd stand the mare one side and the stallion the other and if he was going to exercise his right, the mare would lean to him and say he was alright, or she would smash into the gate and off you'd go and take her away. They'd bring another one out and you'd probably get two that day on that farm. But it was nothing to have perhaps 16 to 20 mares in a day. Twenty six I done one day with Moulton Bellman. That was after the war and Dick Marler from Marsham who'd come back from the war, he rid round with me. Two or three different times he used to come with me for the ride out.

Moulton Bellman (c. late 1940s).

You used to have to book everything then for the Norfolk 'Suffolk Horse Society' and with the booking you had to keep everything: how many mares had been tried and how many had been serviced on each farm. Well, Dick sat in the lorry doing this for me, which was a bonus.

And sometimes the days would end with a few problems to deal with:

We finished up at Springtime Farm at Cawston, five o'clock time. David Lee was the manager there then. Twelve mares they had in that stable. There was an old farmer come into the yard and oh, didn't he want to watch the mares being covered and the performance going on. 'Oh, he hen't done no work today,' he say, 'tha's the first one he's had?'

'No, that bloody well en't,' I said.

'Well, he can't cover no more,' he say. So I said to David, 'Have you still got that old mare – is she still in the stables?' We had tried two or three years but we'd give her up. She'd finished breeding but she was always interested. 'Bring her out, David.'

And the old stallion he got excited and he did the same to her. And Dick sat in the lorry and he booked it – three guineas.

But of course, this was not a genuine charge for a breeding mare, and the confusion in booking this down led to a shortfall of three guineas:

Later on we sat counting this money up and we were frightened we were short. We went through and I was three guineas short and I had got to take the money that night and get everything squared up. We had to rake round and I believe I had to borrow off Edie Fulcher, next door, to make up my three guineas. It was that bloody mare what we had played about with. Dick had booked that you see and that was the day Dick say 'I think you've done enough today Jack, you've done 26 mares since you left home this morning'.

Jack found the business of keeping detailed records in conformity with the Societies' wishes a difficult task.

The stallions of years back were in Jack's opinion greatly superior in terms of breeding.

They used to leave more foals then. They don't now, one here one there. The times I've argued with the top men of the society but they allus got me beat 'cos they used to ask what percentage did I leave. I couldn't answer that because we never kept records in them days, not like they do now. But I said the only consolation I've got is when you've got a farmer customer who's kept using you for 10 years, he was satisfied.

That was when we were at Marsham and that went on for years until the farm got sold. Mr Holman kept the Aylsham Farm, which his son John has got now. I am still friendly with him. That's when I got a council house at Marsham and that's where the three girls were born.

So having another door closed, Jack had to find work wherever it was available:

I had to work anywhere I could get a job – anywhere as long as I had got a pair of hands. You can get work today if you are willing to do it. I'd do anything – mucking pigs out, plucking hens, currant-picking – I'd do anything to earn some money. I'd work anywhere for a month or two. I got onto the aerodrome near Cawston. A big firm from London was demolishing an old hall and everything. I went there cleaning bricks, as general labourer. I was there for several months.

When I come out of Grove Farm, Marsham, and went to Stody, that was just before Rosemarie was born. I used to go into the shop and get a packet of fags, and they had a little teddy bear in there. I asked them to keep that and I paid so much for them to keep it on hold. Blast, I was so pleased I'd got a little daughter.

Jack's wife Margaret had a strange way of warning the family that a baby would soon be on the way:

The Wards lived next door to Nurse Hunt. I always remember biking up the hill to go home teatime and Nurse Hunt was in our yard and she kept beckoning me. She say:

'Don't stop and keep a-talking to me now. You better be a-getting home. I can talk to you later on. I expect I shall be back again afore long. I've been past twice today and both times Margaret has been digging the garden over.' She always did, just before she had children. She always used to go down the road in the evening and smell the muckheap. She just had to go and smell that. It became quite a laugh.

With Jack's growing reputation, there was usually someone who was prepared to recommend him for a job:

Knights of Stody – Suffolk horse people – lent a stallion to the Society to travel for the season. Major Rodwell was secretary for the Society and he knew I was biking backwards and forwards – I used to see him when I was biking. I used to bike there 17 miles morning and night until I got a little old motorbike. He pulled me up and said he was looking for a stallion leader to travel the stallion. Well I didn't take a lot of encouraging and I took that on. I took it on for the 12-week season.

I went on to work at Stody Hall for the Knights family and I was happy doing odd jobs.

He remembers giving a lift on the back of his motor-bike to a man working over in the same direction as himself:

When I was at Stody, going away from Marsham at 20 minutes to seven to go along the Holt Road and across to Wood Dalling then onto Stody, there was a chap lived down the road who used to work at Wood Dalling, which is about half way. For months and months nearly every day of the week we'd click, and he'd hang onto my shoulder and I'd take him all the way there to work. He'd be the first one to work those mornings and he didn't have to bike!

Jack also remembers well his brush with the law when he was riding this untaxed motor-bike!

When I had my motorbike, and 'cos we never had any money in them days, I never had no lights on the bloody thing. For weeks and weeks I used to come home with a bicycle light on the front. Well I come home one night near the Cawston Police House and the policeman stood there waiting for me. An army Land Rover had followed me and he had seen me one or two nights and he had reported me. I got away with it in the finish. 'Course I hadn't got any tax nor nothing, so the next morning I had to get up early and go to Thorpe to tax my motorbike and went and shew him my tax. That was a good old bike that was – a Triumph – one gear down and two up. I used to sit Bryan on the tank and Rosemarie on the back.

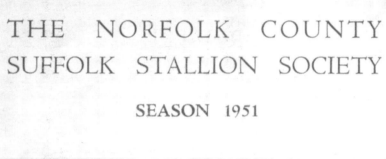

THE NORFOLK COUNTY
SUFFOLK STALLION SOCIETY

SEASON 1951

STODY DRUMMER BOY
(8065)

will travel in the

HOLT, AYLSHAM, ACLE AND
YARMOUTH DISTRICT

The cover of a 'Stallion Season' leaflet (1951): this was given to the farmers to enable them to plan the visits of selected stallions. (Leaflet information overleaf).

THE NORFOLK COUNTY SUFFOLK STALLION SOCIETY

Has hired from

GEO. C. & F. C. KNIGHT, STODY FARMS

THE SUFFOLK STALLION
STODY DRUMMER BOY
(8065)   (Foaled 1948)

Sire—Chessell Guardsman, 7345, by
                Bawdsey Sir Roger, 5970
Dam—Chessell Pearl Anne, 21538, by
                Orwell Beatty, 6258
2nd Dam—Fakenham Pearl, 14177, by
                Fakenham Brocade, 5770
Record to 7th Dam

"Stody Drummer Boy" is a very well-bred, big, weighty, upstanding, red chestnut Stallion, with a lot of bone on good feet, good quarters, and moves well. He won 1st Hunts. County, 4th Royal Norfolk, in 1948; only times that he has been shown.

His Sire "Chessell Guardsman" was Junior and Supreme Champion at the Woodbridge Show as a 3-year-old, and has sired many 1st prize Royal and County Show winners in recent years, and is by that renowned Stallion "Bawdsey Sir Roger."

His Dam "Chessell Pearl Anne" is a County Show winner, and by that noted Stallion "Orwell Beatty."

SERVICE FEE £3 - 10 - 0

All Fees and Subscriptions to be paid to the Groom not later than the FIRST WEEK IN JUNE, for which an Official Receipt will be given.

Cheques to be made payable to the Society

GROOMS FEE 5/-

To be paid to the Groom for all mares tried

SUBSCRIPTION 2/6 per member

No Mare will be tried unless owner pays his Subscription

EVERY CARE WILL BE TAKEN, BUT NEITHER THE SOCIETY NOR THE STALLION OWNER WILL BE RESPONSIBLE FOR ACCIDENTS

A limited number of Assisted Nominations at 35/- will be granted for farmers of less than 100 acres or £100 rent, whose chief living is derived from farming. Applications to the Secretary.

NOTE. The Society is travelling only four Stallions this season as compared with seven in past years. As much of the County as possible will be covered and every effort made to send a stallion to those breeders who require one. *If however, a Stallion should not call at a breeder's premises in the early stages of the season, and the breeder requires a Stallion, will he please communicate with the Secretary.*

H. RODWELL, *Secretary.*

EASTGATE HOUSE, CAWSTON, NORWICH.

Telephone: Cawston 32.

Travelling the stallions was now considerably easier, with the use of a lorry, but Jack's keenness landed him with one show, way up in Scotland:

Information from a 'Stallion Season' leaflet (1951).

I had a little Bedford lorry at Stody. They got me that when I was living at Marsham, to travel their stallion for the season. The Society hired the stallion off of him to do their route. Anyhow they got me to go and help their groom out at the shows. They used to show five or six horses then: two-year old, three-year old, stallion, mare and foal. Big business it was then. When I was living at Marsham, the Suffolk Horse Society they got a fit into their head that they were going to have classes up in Scotland, for Suffolk Horses, at Dundee. Knights had entered two or three. Stody Marigold was one, and a three-year-old Suffolk filly. Knight's brother Fritz was an auctioneer, like himself, in Huntingdon and he used to run his own big shows. He got George Knights, his brother, to patronise him, so he entered Stody Marigold to go to Huntingdon. Then she was entered in Hassocks, down south. I'd got to go to those two places and as it turned out, they were the same week as the Scotland trip.

They (the Society) were running a trainload from Yarmouth, picking up straight through Ipswich – all these people and their horses to make up their classes at the Royal Highland Show in Dundee. I had to go in my Bedford lorry (lovely little lorries they were). I had got to go to Huntingdon on the

Wednesday and the Thursday, and then I had to go down to Hassocks for the Friday and Saturday. How we used to find our way I don't know. This was also when petrol was rationed and coupons were like gold dust. On the Saturday afternoon I'd got to leave there and find my way up to Dundee ready for Monday morning.

I got permission off the Society people at Hassocks to skip the parade, as it wasn't until four or five o'clock. It was always the last thing in them days, so people could see all the animals in the parade. I got off with my little lorry and I got up into Yorkshire that night looking for somewhere to sleep. I saw a place with some rails and paddocks that looked like a horsey place, drove in and explained what I needed. They said it was alright, so I put the horse into the stable, put my bed up in the lorry and got out my little stove and had my supper there.

Off I set the next morning for Dundee. Half past six time, when I was on the road, the first big garage I see that was open I pulled up to fill up with petrol. I'd got a pocketful of coupons through Knights, because they were auctioneers and had got a business. I went to pay and they didn't want the coupons! Well, I got enough to run my motorbike for I don't know how long, 'cos you see you were only allowed so much petrol a month for your motorbike and you had to use that careful like. The reason they didn't want the coupons was because petrol had gone off ration at midnight! I didn't know because I hadn't had communication with anybody. Anyway I found the showground and got there six o'clock Sunday night.

But having travelled all the way north, luck was against Jack and his horse.

Monday morning they were all there. Some of them had got there Saturday afternoon. They got onto the showground and got their respective boxes or stables, whatever you like to call them. That gave them time to get their animals ready for Tuesday morning, which was the first show-day. Anyhow I got onto the showground and the horse was lame from too much travelling. I pailed her with water and ice, swamped her all night to get that leg down. I got into the ring and Mr Philip Woodward from Stowmarket was judging. I walked her up and walked her back, like you do in front of the judges. When I got to the end the judge's steward he came across and said, 'in the judge's opinion your horse is lame. Now you can quietly take her out of the ring or you will have to go to the back of the class.' He was quite right of course, so I took her out. It was the Norfolk Show at Keswick the next week and I knew if I could get her home for two or three days, I could get her right to win the Norfolk.

Being in Scotland was like being in a foreign country for Jack. And before he left he had an experience with a pony, followed by a strange coincidence:

The job I had there, 'cos they were Scottish up there and they spoke a different language! I used to ring mother up at eight o'clock at night. I'd made arrangements to stay with a little farm just down the road that used to cost half a crown. This night one of my mates said to me, 'You're always up early Jack. I've left a pail of water out – can you give it to my horse?' You always water your horse first afore you feed them, that way you got the water on the stomachs first, before they're fed, then they didn't have anymore till dinnertime. I'll tell you the reason why. In nature (you see it on the television on these nature programmes) you see the herd of horses first thing and they will gallop miles to go to water. Then they stand and have a good drink and they'll have no more till the next morning.

Well anyhow, that night I slept in the lorry. About half past three or four o'clock time – the first thing you do as soon as you open your eyes is to go water and feed your horses. Something woke me up, bloody horses a-banging. There was a little dun pony, 13 hand, lovely looking little dun – a little stallion, and he'd got out. He was running up and down snorting and upsetting the other horses, shrieking and whatnot! So I had to get a rope and catch him. I knew two or three rows down (we were all in our own section) there was a whole row of boxes with this type of breed in. The door was open to his stable so I put him in there, tied the door all up again and settled everything down.

You had to stop the week then. I had a hell of a job to get written permission to leave before the parade. I had to have a vet and that sort of thing to say it was best to get her home. I got away that night at five o'clock when they let me off.

I'd come as far as a place called Airdrie and that was getting dusk and I was looking for somewhere to stay. You always find horsey places, and they couldn't be more helpful. The week before, the pilgrims that come down here to Walsingham had stayed there. Anyway I got the horse stabled and got my little stove going when somebody came out to see if everything was all right. She said, 'We've got food laid on, you come in.' So I went in and sat in their fairly big room and all round the room were pictures of these dun ponies. I always remember 'cos l was polite in them days.

I said, 'I beg your pardon, ma'am, but this fella is on the Royal Showground ain't he?'
'Yes, he is,' she said, 'they've had a good day up there.'
I said, 'He was out last night upsetting all the horses. I caught him and put him back in his box.' They knew because the box door had been broken and tied up again and one thing and another. Now what a coincidence. I had breakfast in the house and set off for home.

Then the next week I was at the Norfolk Show at Keswick, 'cos that used to be scattered about, the Norfolk Show did. That was at Sandringham one year or Beccles another year.

It was at Marsham that Jack had his first car – and his first accident!

We had an old-fashioned London taxi. It had a driver's seat with a platform where the others (passengers) used to go in, and in the back you could sit four or five people. It was luxury. I used to use it then because Hewitt found me that, and I used to go backwards and forwards to the farm at Stratton Strawless. What stick in my mind are that the tyres on it were smooth.

Anyhow, I was going to the Ipswich Show and was staying overnight and packed my things up and was going round South Walsham on my way to pick the stallion up. I was going round some sharp old bends there and they were on a slope. I was going about 25 miles an hour and it had been pouring with rain. It was Yarmouth Races day and there was a lot of traffic went down that road. You got a lot of rubber on the road, and that motor slid and rolled over and over and when I did manage to get out, the engine was still a running. I went and pulled the leads off the battery and the whole windscreen came out and lay on the verge and it hadn't broke. Cars came round and come to help and we rolled it over and put the screen in the back. I had to jump on the mudguards and got them sort of ship-shape and put the leads on the battery and finished my journey.

But the old taxi was probably not quite suitable for transporting freshly-baked tarts!

We were going home to see my mother and father at Reymerston in that old taxi and Margaret had made a big tart and she had laid it in the well where you put the luggage. Coming through Mattishall and Tuddenham we saw an old man on the side of the road feeding his donkey. Well that was something for him, weren't it – to see this taxi. He stood there gawking and I pulled slowly up to him and I asked him:
'Could you tell me the way to London?'
Time I was a-talking to him the donkey stuck its head through the window to the girls. Anyhow further down the road I swung round a corner messing about, and shot the bloody tart onto the road! I think we had to get out and rescue some of that.

Jack also remembers a family outing to Yarmouth on a very blustery night:

I remember when we went to Yarmouth to go and see the last night of the lights. I come home from work and it was a filthy night. It was raining and the wind was strong. I got the girls in the back with a Tilly lamp. We were in the taxi going up the Acle straight and the wind, that blew across there! They had to lie down to keep out of it. We went all the way along the sea front down to the harbour mouth and then we came out the back way along the river and all the ships there were lit up. There was a big one with a lot of lights on, so we pulled up and got out and walked along. We could see the captain and they were having their tea. We stopped on the way home and we all had fish and chips. That was an outing. That was something in those days. We were the only ones in the parish that had a car, and that was only through scrimping and saving and earning an extra shilling where I could.

Around this time they also had an old van – with a make-shift roof:

We went to Watford in that old van with three girls in it and it hadn't got a roof in it. Mother went down to Aylsham and bought some of that 'Contact' stuff – it was a new stuff out – you could stick it on table-tops and so on. She went and got a roll of that and we spent no end of time putting that on the roof so we had a roof on. Well we just got over Thetford Heath when the wind got underneath and blew it off into the air.

We got to Denmark Street and it was a big occasion, so we had to park in the street. Sister Hilda's husband George, he was most particular. I can see him now making sure I was in the right place. He didn't notice there was no tax on the damn thing.

When the family eventually left Marsham there were few dry eyes. They left many good friends behind:

There was the Fulchers – we used to have to come through his garden down a path into our garden. They were good people – good old sorts, like Aunt Edie and Uncle Evan. That was when we should have won the football pools! Uncle Evan used to sort that out and help me fill the football pools in. He came over six o'clock and told us we'd won, but of course we hadn't, because the coupon still sat on the mantelpiece. I hadn't sent it in because I hadn't got any money to buy the postal order.

That day we moved out of Marsham to go to Upton (near Acle) there was tears all down the street, that is the truth. There were people waving and crying as we left, but that was village life then.

Jack with the family visiting his sister Hilda in Watford (no tax on the van!) The photo was taken in the 1950s.

THE MARSHES

The move across to Upton near Acle was a long way, with a different kind of country-side to work:

I went to Hewitt's and they had Suffolk horses there. I had Worstead Monogram then. They had the biggest new horsebox off Mann Egerton – there was quite a do about that. While I was there I think we were one of the first ones to plough the marshes up to grow wheat. I had an International tractor and the wheat was so high and the thistles, you had to stand up on the tractor sometimes to see your way through. I think we were the ones that pioneered the combine on the marsh with a Claas combine. It was only a little old thing with a bagger on the back. Bryan – he would be about 15 or 16 – used to stand on the back and bag the corn into 16 stone sacks. He used to tie them up and he'd get about four on the plat-form and then he'd pull a string and a shute would put them off in the field. Then the other workers on the farm had to come along and manhandle them onto the cart and take them home. There were several combines about, but we were the first ones on the marshes.

In them days different farmers would grow as heavy a crop as they could, even if they had to sell as second rate for feeding. Hewitt always had a system. He would grow malt barley and when that was passed as 100% malting barley it was worth a lot of money. Bull and Norket (?) from Kings Lynn were the biggest buyers of malting barley and they used to buy it off Hewitts in corn sacks. If it wasn't quite what they wanted he used to put it into a heap and cover it over with a tarpaulin and make it sweat a bit to get it right.

And Jack now became involved in the 'haulage' business for farms:

Anyhow, Hewitt had got two lorries on haulage and they would come and take it on haulage so he used to get a lot of contracts for carting corn and barley. They used to go and buy the crop from various people and then they would send them a letter to say the haulage people would collect it and deliver it to them, so it was then out of the farmers' hands.

The next order he got was to deliver to Bullard's brewery in Norwich. I took the first load in and backed the lorry under the shute. Then the chain would come down and you would wrap that round the sack. He'd press a button and that would lift that up through the lid. He'd take that up and shoot that out and then the sack would come down on the chain and you would unload the lorry like that.

Worsted Monogram: at the time of the photo the horse was six years old; it weighed, approximately 19 hundredweight and was 16 hands high. It was let to the Suffolk Stallion Society for three seasons.

Worstead Monogram from Hewitt's of Upton, (c.1955–6).

Jack thought about the system of buying and selling, and felt he could make things work a little better!

Time I was unloading, the man came down out of the office with his trilby on and asked for a sample. Then he asked for another sample out of another sack. He wanted to know where that had come from. Anyway I had to go up to the office to get the tickets signed and we got talking about this sample of corn and I told him:

'I can't make out why you don't buy off the farm 'cos that come off the farm where I work and there are two or three more stacks there. Why don't you come and buy it direct off the farm, which means you would be cutting the middle man out?'

He said, 'That's a good idea, but we can't rely on that, because we have to have a regular supply. If there is bad weather wintertime the farmers can't thrash the stack. We have to have our regular consignment every day of the year and we must keep up production. We rely on the middleman to keep us supplied.'

I went home that night and went down to the pub with brother Bob (he lived next door to us then). I stood in the passage of the pub and got talking to the landlord. He brought me one of those old blue bags that sugar used to come in, with some corn in. I had a look and he said that a local firm had offered him so and so for that. I told him, 'I've now been delivering corn for about a pound a coomb more than that. Don't you sell that! Can I take this sample with me?'

I took it with me the next morning and shew the man at the brewery and he asked where he could contact the owner? I went straight home and on the way phoned the landlord up and said:

'You've got a man coming to see you this afternoon about the corn.'

Anyhow he got a pound a coomb more, and when he next saw me he give me five pound and he told me to go up the farm and see his brother who'll also give me a fiver. That was TEN pounds! I kept all the tip money I got and still lived off my wage.

Dealing with horses on this marshland area was at times quite different work and Jack also had to help deal with foreign buyers.

When you went down to the marshes and the cattle came down to see you, they would come galloping across and you could feel the water under the grass because the grass was on top of the water. Once we had a load of Pakistani people come over to this country and they wanted to buy female Suffolks to take home to cross-breed with their riding horses. They bought six and they had all got to be 16 hands, not over.

Anyhow we got them down ready, and then we bought a two-year old registered stallion off Berty Balls of Seething to go with them so they were in foal before they went. We had to have them measured by one of their people and we got down onto the marsh and kept catching these horses to be measured. When the man measured them he got a tape measure out and he started to go in and out. I say, 'You can't do that, you just go straight up the leg and straight up to the shoulder.' Anyway, we got them all done and they were ready to go.

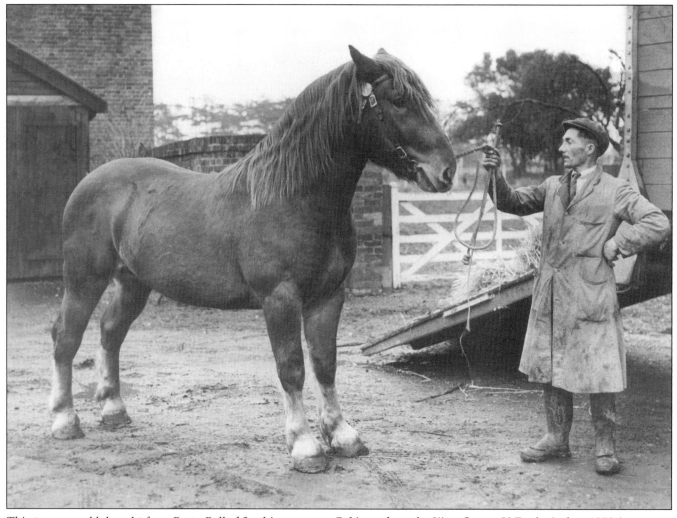

This two-year old, bought from Berty Ball of Seething, went to Pakistan from the King George V Docks (c. late 1950s).

Raveningham Molly on the right and Raveningham Bessie on the left (c. 1950s) The latter mare died on the boat to Pakistan. Bryan is on the right and Kenny on the left.

Alfred Hewitt of Upton, Jack's boss for a time.

Two year old Upton Diagram exported to Pakistan by Alfred Hewitt.

Fred Shearing, on the right, at the Royal Norfolk Show, with the mare Bawdsey Lure and the foal Raveningham Bessie.

At the Norfolk showground with Jack's son Bryan, (fifth from the front) aged about 14; the mare is Bawdsey Lure.

And Jack became used to the strange behaviour of certain stallions:

There was that stallion who, when he was on the marsh with the mares, he kept putting them into the dykes. We had to take the lorry and go down there one night and had to keep getting these mares out of the dyke by moonlight. In the end we cornered the stallion. He got in a state and went into the dyke, so we haltered him up and took him home, otherwise he would have been putting mares in and out of the dyke all night long.

In them days, March and April time, it was nothing for people to take a bunch of cattle down onto the marsh and run them into the dykes. Once they had been in once, you see, they would be frightened and wouldn't go in again. It was an old dodge to cure them, and it did.

The extra cash being earned even allowed the family to buy one of the first televisions:

I used to do a lot of carting for different people then, corn carting, cattle carting, that was how we had our first television and that cost £72. We bought it from Snelling of Blofield. Farmers had television but there weren't many farm-workers who did! When Mr Snelling came to deliver the television he couldn't believe it because he had brought all the paper work for H.P. and I paid him in pound notes. That would be about 1957.

Preparing horses for sale, plaiting-up, is a skilful job, and Jack became expert at it:

I used to cart corn for different people – and sugar beet. Jack Allen from the 'Kings Arms', he was a proper old-fashioned landlord. They had a farm down at Upton and his brother lived on the farm. It was a family affair and they give you a tip. Then there would be Michaelmas sale come up in the paper in October with various other sales. They would have horses for sale, and the auctioneers used to book me in to plait the tails up for when they were sold. I'd pick up a couple of quid here and there. There was a row of trees outside the saleroom and we had an old wagon rope. As they came into the sales you'd tie them up and do their tails – some of them with tails down to the ground. Some of them were a bit naughty because they had never had much done with them. One sale there were 27 horses, and that meant another few quid for me.

Jack was always prepared to do that little extra it seems, where the chance of earning a pound or two offered itself:

I remember these sales – the cattle market on a Thursday at Acle. One auctioneer would be one side and another one the other side, and they would sell all sorts – cattle, pigs and poultry. There had been a strike on, a miners' strike I think, and the cattle weren't making anything 'cos no one hadn't got any money. No one was buying the beef. Anyhow, they had got a lot of nice little black cattle in the big yard he wanted to be getting rid of, and I took about six of them down to the sale yard. I went to back-up, to unload and go to the sale, and Dick Wharton, the auctioneer, (he was a gentleman he was), he said,

'Morning Juby, what have you here for us this morning? I tell you there'll be some trading done this morning, the strike is all off! You haven't got another lot like that, have you?'

I said, 'There's a yard full!'

I was too late to get them back to his sale because his started at ten o'clock, but the other one started at one o'clock. I pulled up with the lorry and went round the corner to a little chap in the office there, Pat, who did the booking-in and I said:

'Do you want another half a dozen cattle?'

'Yes,' he say, 'we hen't got too many in today Jack.'

I rang up the farm straightaway and said:

'Pick out another half-a-dozen cattle. I shall be home afore long and take another load.'

That was how things were. A lot of lorry drivers would have sat and had a cup of tea and not have bothered, but I had an interest in it.

When the local Royal Norfolk Show allowed, attendance became a Juby family affair, and over the years the hospitality from their improvised horsebox home became legendary:

It was when I was still at Hewitt's when they had the Royal Norfolk Show at Norwich and Mavis was a toddler. Hewitt had got two or three horses there and that was when the picture was in the *Eastern Daily Press*. I'd come from Hewitt's and you had the horses there for a week. I went home on the Monday morning and said to Mother 'pack your things up!' She had to get one of the girls away from school, and we packed all the pots and pans up and we stopped the week at the Royal Norfolk Show. I had got a spare horsebox because you would enter four and only take three and so on.

First thing I would always do is put nails round the box so you could hang up cups and mugs and saucepans. There would be a little old stove to make a cup of tea. We'd put straw down with blankets and that is where you would sleep. Dick Jeeves from the *EDP*, he come there and took the picture. He reached over the door and mother stood there pouring a cup of tea, with Mavis asleep on the floor. The picture was on the *EDP* stand at the show.

The next morning Mr Philip Woodward, president of the show then, came round and said:

'Morning Jack, I understand you have got your family here with you?'

I thought I was going to get wrong for having the horsebox, so I introduced him to mother and he had a little chat with the girls. Then he said to me:

'I will take your wife with me.'

He took her up to the grandstand and he introduced her to the people there and told them that this lady and her children can come into the grandstand at anytime. I thought that was very nice of him.

It is surprising the people used to come round and have a cup of tea. They used to like to have a china cup and saucer. She must have made gallons of tea then, and they got so they expected it over the course of the years.

Improvised accommodation in a horse-box at the Royal Norfolk Show in the 1950s. Note the bone china cups and saucers and ribbons in the hair.

But life was still changing for Jack, and a move nearer his roots was to happen. He was to work for the Peacock family again:

I met Geoffrey Peacock up at the cattle market one Saturday when he had got the big farm at Morley. He said he had got a house he was going to modernize and he wanted me to move in there. So I left Hewitt's and went there – that was when Mavis was a toddler.

Margaret (on the far right) used to attend all the shows and provided meals and endless cups of tea. She would clean all the brasses and iron all the ribbons.

7

LIME TREE FARM

So Jack moved his family to Morley St Botolph, near Wymondham, to work for Geoffrey Peacock, furthering his interest in the showing and the sale of horses to all parts of the world:

Geoffrey, he sold a stallion to two brothers in Africa through the Society. What we used to do was take pictures with a little old Kodak camera – both sides, front end and back end. When you do that sort of thing, you want them so you just get the four legs on both sides and they can see all the way down the legs. Then we had to send the mother's and father's pedigree over – along with what they had done and what he had done, and all the paperwork. They finished up buying the stallion, which came from Lime Brocade. I had to go down to Ware. He had to stand down there three weeks in quarantine. Three years later we had a letter from the brothers stating what the horse had done and they wanted a replacement. So we sold them another stallion.

Another three years went by and the brothers ordered their third horse. In ten years they had bought three stallions. The last horse was Histon Interloper:

He was a bit naughty! When we lived down at 'Meadowlands', the girls used to go onto the meadow to pick primroses, and play. Anyway he'd let you on the meadow but he wouldn't let you off! They used to have to stand and wait for me to go home for dinner before they could get off! He was the one who used to stand and watch our television at night. We went up the lane one night to go to Granny Juby's and mother made us go back and put the television on for him because she had forgot to draw the curtains back so he could watch the television!

It was one of the conditions of this African sale, amazingly, that the horse had to win Supreme Championship at the 'Royal'.

I was at the Royal Show on the Tuesday morning at 11 o'clock. I was in the ring with Histon Interloper, patting him on the neck as we went in for the Supreme Championship. A young chap on a motorbike dressed in red things and a red bag on him had been up and down the stables looking for Peacock's Percherons. We had got a telegram from Africa confirming the deal – providing he won our English Royal Show. This deal had been going on for weeks and weeks and that happened within minutes like that. He had just won the Royal!

Anyhow, they bought this horse. I had to take him to King George V Docks, Liverpool to put him on the boat. They put him in a crate and that is where he had to stand. They had slings underneath him so they could take the weight off him to rest him every so often. He was the one who bit a man's finger off who was looking after him on the boat.

Above: *Jack and his brother Bob took one stallion and two fillies to Prestwick airport in April 1976 for shipment to Canada. The crates had to be built around the horses to give them the correct space.*

Above, right: *Jack always ensured his horse's comfort before a flight – and his tigers!*

That was when Roey (Rosemarie) went with me to Liverpool. She went for a ride. She was only a little girl, and I made a bed of straw up in the back of the lorry for her to have a sleep on the way home. I had to be home by eight o'clock that night so mother could go to work – night work up at Wicklewood Hospital.

I said to Roey: 'There is a great old iron bar in there. When you wake up, just bang on the door and I will stop. Well, in a queue of traffic – the police were stopping traffic for something – as the policeman came up to my window she hacked on that cubby hole door. Blast, he didn't half jump!

We got letters back from these brothers. They wrote and told us how they got on with him and Mrs Peacock (Senior) she was ever so pleased.

Jack emphasised the importance of 'showing' in the exposure the horses received:

This was only through showing. We had a mare called Hempnall Annie and she bred several foals; it was one of her foals that we lost down on Acle marshes. That was when showing was a business. She had been champion every time we went to a show except the last time, when she was reserve champion. We bred out of her, but she could have been on a meadow somewhere. If she hadn't have been shown, nobody wouldn't have wanted to know. If there hadn't been any write-up about her then she would never have been noticed. That was how business was then. We kept her on when she packed up breeding, and she ended up with bad legs – arthritis or something like that – and had to be put down.

Above: *Hempnall Annie was the first horse Roger Peacock bought. She had several foals, of which most went abroad. One of her foals ended up in a dyke on the marshes.*

Left: *Hempnall Annie at the Loddon Show.*

Jack remembers that sad loss of one of her foals:

One of her foals – it was a big mare – ended up dying down on Acle marshes in a dyke. She was right down in the marshes and Geoffrey (Peacock) came into the yard with a message that a horse was in a dyke. So we took shovels, picks and ropes and went down there. It was about three mile across these marshes, through gateways. Weren't that a job to get down there! She was right on the last marsh against the bank by the river, where the boats all go through Breydon Water. She was in this dyke and there she was just trying to keep her nostrils out of the water.

Two marsh-men were there and in them days you used to have to dig the bank beside her, and dig a hole to let the water out so it would come round her – so you could get to see her legs. We got the rope onto her and we'd put an anchor in a crowbar in the marsh as far as you could get, so you had got an anchor. You'd put the rope round that then you'd half a loop in the rope half way up and bring it round the anchor. Then you'd put that back though the loop and that way you'd got three purchases then. That's how we slid her out, poor old bugger, as far as we could. You can pull a lot of them out down there and they would get up and shake themselves and go galloping off – but she didn't. She had been right in and she had been in there a long time. You have to get them as far away as quick as you can, away from the dyke, 'cos when they get up, if they are weak, they stagger and fall in again. So we pulled her away as far as we could by hand, but she hadn't got any life in that leg. There was nothing there.

We had to get the vet out from Yarmouth – Mr Moult.(?) He had to come down from Yarmouth by train and get off on the railway line. There's what you call whistle stop – you'd pull the whistle and the train would stop! He got off the train and come across the marshes and he injected with various things but that was never going to work. Anyway I said to Geoffrey,
'I 'm NOT – I'm not leaving her laying there! That en't that long ago I had her in the ring winning the championship, patting her on the neck as pleased as punch – so I'm *not* leaving her here!'
'Oh well,' he say, 'tha's my hoss and I'm not going to stop with her.' And he went home.

That's when I kept pigs on the meadow and I was worrying about them being fed. He went home and see mother and she give him one of my big old coats and a bottle of hot drink. He bought me some fags and he come back with the car as far as he could. Roger brought the Mini for me. What a night! I can hear it now. I was right against the wall. There's a bloody great wall going down beside Breydon Water, into Yarmouth! Whoosh, whoosh, whoosh! That water kept up against those walls all night. I sat there in a thick fog with the old mare and every now and again she have a struggle to get up. That got to nearly daylight and I knew then there was no hope of her struggling to get up. I suppose it was half past five – six o'clock. I had to go across to the Mini 'cos they couldn't get it close to me. So I walked across there over the plank across the dyke and got into the car and come home. I got into Lime Tree Farm yard at quarter to seven, straight into the yard, pipped my hooter and made a noise – you used to start work at seven. Geoffrey looked out of the bedroom window and he says:

'What's happened?'

I said, 'You'd better get on the phone onto the slaughterer, and tell him to get down there and put her out of her misery.'

'As bad as that,' he said, 'You're sure?'

'Yes,' I said, 'Don't let her suffer no longer. She's had it, she's finished. She might even be dead now. He's got to go and pick her up, so get him down there as soon as he can, and shoot her.'

'Oh, oh,' he say, 'Well what are you going to do now?' That was getting on for seven.

I say, 'I'm going to get home now, and have a wash and a cup of tea.'

'Oh alright,' he said.

We used to leave off at 11 on a Saturday, and he told me that I could take a fork and matches and go burning the straw up against the church, at the back of the shop- that's when we used to burn straw in them days. So I filled the morning up burning the straw. This was Saturday morning.

The system of payment in those days was hard, but in Jack's eyes fair. The same description could be applied to his boss.

The next Thursday night was pay night. All during 'haysell' (haytime) and harvest we'd do two-and-a-half hours overtime. We were all allowed the same time and were allowed 20 minutes for a cup of tea if we stopped that full time. When I went up the door to get my money I said:

'What about Friday night?'

He says, 'What do you mean, what about Friday night? You didn't expect me to pay you for sitting down there did you?'

'No,' I said, 'but if I had been at home, I should have been like these other chaps and got my two and a half hours in.'

'Well alright,' he says, 'I'll grant you that.'

So he paid me the two-and-a-half hours. That was acceptable then, that was the thing them days, you see. They had to be hard 'cos things were hard then, but I chose to stay down there with the horse. He didn't ask me, did he? But I *wouldn't* leave my horse.

I'm telling you how hard times were and how hard people were, and I'm not being critical because that was the times, and things were hard. But Geoffrey was noted for being hard, and everything had to be exact, not a ha' penny less, nor a ha' penny more.

A family trip round the coast on one occasion led to a business trip further afield:

We used to – (I always say 'we' because I always looked on the farm as mine, in my mind') – we used to sell horses to Vaux's Brewery, up in Sunderland. They had several horses off us. All the breweries had horses to cart the beer and they did it all with Percheron horses. They had geldings (these were three or four year-old castrated horses) ready to go into the towns. They had to be bred specially. They didn't breed their own because they hadn't the facilities to breed them in the middle of the town. We always found them two or three whenever they wanted them. I remember one day I had got the girls in a little old motor and we went round by the coast. I used to get a fit sometimes – when I had got half a crown for petrol and we used to have a little ride out. I went round by Bacton to a farm I used to go to – Mrs Wing – Percheron people. I pulled up to look at the horses out on the meadow – lovely grey horses. Time I was looking at them an old boy came along on his bike.

'Hello Jack, what are you doing about here? You want to tell your governor to come and buy the horses. She's packing up. She isn't going to breed any more 'cos the tractors are getting about.'

Geoffrey come down to Meadowland Cottage Sunday night. He mostly came down and had a chat, but he said:
'I don't want to know about any more horses – there's enough about here now. They aren't a-paying.'
He always reckoned nothing was paying.

Anyhow on the following Wednesday I come home from Bury sugar-beet factory and he asked,
'What permits you got? How many hosses can you get on that lorry Jack? They are big hosses!' He'd been and bought them!

He rang Sunderland up and they came down – brought a vet, a manager and a head horseman. They stayed at the Abbey Hotel for the night so they could inspect these horses. I had to run them up and down the yard and up the road, then they had a little conference. They wanted this one and that one, they had to get matching horses – they couldn't have one dark and the other one lighter, same size heads etc. Anyhow, they bought three.

After the show: Jack and stallion admiring the rosette.

So obviously this required a long trip north with the horses. Initially it was too snowy, but then Jack was prepared to go – with some company.

We were snowed in for a while then, and Geoffrey wouldn't let me go until the weather broke. He came out one afternoon and he say to me, 'If you can get the other side of Hingham and Watton, the AA say it is all clear and you will have no problem.
'What time will you be going?' he say.
'I shall be loading up half past two – three o'clock time, in the morning, on Friday.'
'Well, is anybody going with you?' he says. 'Jack, it's bad old weather. I never get away from the farm. Can I come for a ride?'
'I shall have to be away by three,' I say, 'It's 262 miles to Sunderland, to the brewery.'

Watering the horses at the pond at Lime Tree Farm. Roger Peacock is on the right.

Lime Anna, one of Roger Peacock's Percherons at Lime Tree Farm, Morley St Botolph, being led in by Jack. An atmospheric shot, now a moment of farming history.

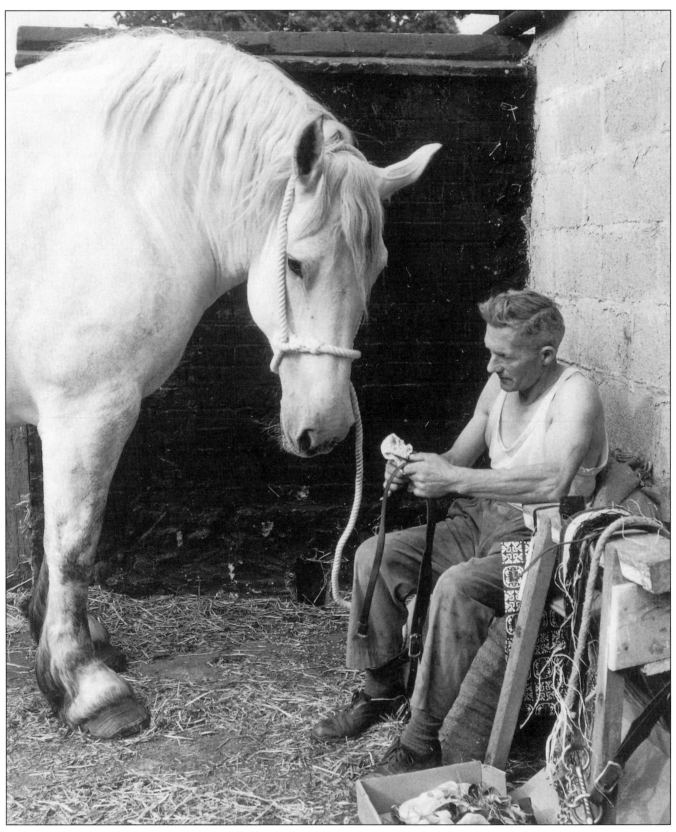

Jack cleaning horse-brasses with the horse looking on.

Dick Jeeves Collection

I'd got an old Dodge petrol-driven lorry with bucket seats and the engine in the middle of them. We got to the other side of Newark on the A1 about daylight. We pulled into a lay-by and had a cup of coffee and what we'd got packed up. He'd got a bag of sweets and a bottle of lemonade. We got out of the lorry and checked the horses through the trap door and we got to Sunderland to the brewery, at 12 o'clock. We got the horses off into their stables. Away come Dickerson, head of the brewery. Vaux's were a noted brewery. He took us up into their restaurant and we had a jolly good meal. Then he wanted to take us down onto the sea front but Geoffrey declined the offer and said, 'I think my driver wants to be getting back.'

'Well anyway,' Mr Dickerson says, 'There's a 19-year old mare down there. She's bad on her hocks and I don't like to see that in the streets. But she's too good to dispose of. Would you like to take her and see if you can breed a foal from her?' He gave Geoffrey the mare!

Coming back we pulled up somewhere and had a cup of tea, five o'clock time, and he bought me ten Players.
'Don't you ever tell my brother Percy or Will Turner and them I've bought you fags.' 'Cos he hated smoking.

They were bucket seats in that lorry and on the way home he say every now and again, 'I suppose you want another one of them fags?' Anyway I'd come 20 or 30 mile further then suddenly something hit me – there was a silence! Blast! For a moment I thought I'd left him at that café. I looked across and he'd slid off the seat into the well of the lorry! Well, when he did come to, he struggled up and got into the seat, and weren't he a bloody misery? Oh weren't he ill, oh weren't he bad? He'd got indigestion.
'Not what you get Jack – I've got it all over my body!'

He was that worried. 'Course he hadn't got indigestion – he had been doubled up in the well, hadn't he! Well, he went off to sleep again. We went down past the church, round past the shop and up into the farmyard and he woke up and he says: 'What, are we home at Morley?' He looked at his watch and said, "It's half past 11. Is this still Friday? All that way Jack, and home again the same day? You hen't bin to sleep hev yer?'
I say, 'Bloody good job for you I hen't!'
'About tomorrow morning,' he say, 'You hen't got no beet, have you? You can have a lay in!'

But Jack didn't want a 'lay in'. And when it came to sorting out the payment for his time, the deductions had to be accepted as 'right', hard as it seems. It was the way of the time.

Next morning it was pouring with rain and the lorry stood in the yard. Mother hadn't called me and it was eight o'clock. Blast I was riled and tore off up that farm. I weren't having people say I had to have a lay in. In those days that would hurt me to say I'd got to have a lay in. Up I go into the yard and pulled up by the dog kennel. He stopped me in the yard,
'Come you here Jack, I've got your money ready, as far as I can,' he said. 'Yesterday there was so many hours overtime on that day. But we stopped half

an hour on the road for breakfast, we had two hours at the brewery for dinner and half an hour for a cup of tea on the way home. You're an hour late this morning, so that's four hours.'

That's what he stopped me for. I'd found the horses and delivered them up there safe and sound, hadn't I, and brought a free one home for him. I went home and sat in the kitchen lunchtime and was telling mother and Kenny, the youngest boy. He sat there listening and he said
'That en't right, father, is it? What did you say?'
'I never said nothing,' I said, ' 'cos he *was* right.'

In them days you kept your mouth shut. There were four or five people in the parish in them days who would have had my job so you kept your mouth shut. We were all in the same boat.

When it was time for the sugar-beet to be lifted and carted to the Bury factory, Jack soon earned a reputation for having the fastest turn-around time going. And of course Jack was also up to any scheme to save him time:

I stood and put sugar-beet onto that lorry – seven ton of beet off a heap on the side of the road – all by hand, with a fork! I had my braces turned down and the sweat has run down into my boots. Up at Wood Lane when I worked for Peacocks, I've done lorry load and lorry load down there. You'd drop your side of the lorry down, do one side and then turn the lorry round and do the other side. I've been to Bury beet factory with a queue from here to London waiting to be washed off. Jack, he wouldn't do that, he'd just go up the ramp and pull up agin the big silos. They were frightening. Get as close as you could. There were sleepers, and you'd crawl along there and let the side down and there would be a lot go off already, and then shovel the rest off down into the hole rather than wait and be washed off. Do the sides up and then come off home ready to do another load.

Poor old Ray Reynolds that worked there, he was like me, he'd got a family. Bloody hard worker. He used to say to me: 'Can't you have a break-down Jack, have a breakdown and come home late tonight,' he'd say, 'and I'll come out there and load your beet with a hurricane light for half a crown'. Get another permit! I was a bugger for getting another permit. You were allowed ten permits. The bigger farms were allowed 20 on certain days, to take the beet in. I had a knack of getting permits – extra permit so you could get your beet in afore we got frosty weather. That was something.

I used to go down to that office, up the steps and tap on the window. There'd be two or three sitting about there. I used to say to them, 'When you see my pretty little face at this window and there en't nothing doing, just ignore me. Don't even bother to get up.' I've took a load in, unloaded and weighed out, set the lorry on the side, gone into the office and they've said, 'Oh hang you on a minute.' The manager here, Mr Tidy, I've seen him go up the ramp and have a look, and perhaps over-night number 2 or number 3 silo would be getting empty, so he'd panic. He wouldn't let the beet get low over-night 'cos it was 24-hour round the clock there. He couldn't run out of beet could he? He'd go into the office and say, 'Can you do another one today? What about tomorrow?'

'Yea I can do another one tomorrow.' They were like gold dust. I've met Colin Downes and my brother Bob.
'Is anything a doing,' they'd say, 'Have you now been down there?'
'Yea,' I'd say, 'I've just got one changed from Saturday morning 'cos I'm cattle-carting Saturday'. Some of them would go down and swear like hell at the people in the office. It was nothing to do with them. I committed murder down that factory for years, for Peacock.

Then when you had to go and get pulp, you had to have it in bags. Well them bags don't come off 100 per cent. Sometimes they'd be a few pound short or a few pound over, and when you went on the weigh bridge you'd be over and they wouldn't let you off. You'd got to go back again and queue and take it off and then it was only guess work weren't it? Sometimes you could bugger about there all day getting the right weight.

I had the knack and I was the turnip king in Bury for years! We used to sow these turnips by ear. Three weeks before you cut the corn, these little turnips would come up, lovely little vegetable turnips, blue but white inside. I used to take a bag-full of them and tuck them in front of the lorry, in the front with the sugar beet. So when you went in with the lorry to take the sample the chaps up there used to lean over and take the turnips. They used to go crazy over them. They even took them home and put them in the deep freezers for Christmas. Every time I went in, well, I was selling Peacocks turnips – one hundredweight at a time, the same price as sugar beet. I used to get away with murder.

I come home from Bury beet-factory one day and I was tied for time so I pulled up and went into the phone box and phoned up to say,
'Send somebody up there to Wood Lane. I shall be home in twenty five minutes. I've got another permit and I shall need some help to get that loaded up so I can be back to the factory this afternoon.'

Interestingly, Jack noted that Geoffrey Peacock remembered that small item of a fourpenny phone-call, when payday came round!

Geoffrey came down to Meadowland Cottage about an hour later and I went to the door. He says:
'I look after you like a father. You are short on your money this week aren't you?'
'I don't know,' I say, 'The money is still in my pocket.'
'Well didn't you phone me from Thetford the other day? That cost you fourpence, didn't it?'
He had brought the fourpence down. He weren't going to have me say to him on the Saturday morning – in front of five or six of them – that he didn't pay me for the phone call. He was like that – right was right and he was a hard but fair man.

Friday night we got our pay. When I was working for Peacocks 11 of us used to go up to Geoffrey Peacock's door. He use to sit there and tear little pieces of paper off out of a little note book. When he had worked out our hours – I never could make out how he done that – they used to double up. Two half crowns is five shillings, two five shillings is 10 shillings – that's how they worked your money out, but they were always right.

Jack also remembers Geoffrey's principles over money being rigidly enforced when he refused to accept delivery of a combine, before the money had been paid:

Geoffrey Peacock went to Coventry with Larkmans, the factory people. They'd got a bus-load of farmers interested in seeing these machines made at the Massey Ferguson works. He came home and said he'd bought this big bagging combine. 'I don't know how we are going to get it about here.' Anyway months later away come a low-loader with a massive combine on. The driver stopped overnight at Larkmans and delivered that the next morning – I can see that as if it was clear as day. Geoffrey came out and he say, 'What have we got here, my man? If you don't mind, my man, can you hang on here a little while?' He wanted to wait until Larkmans opened and he went and saw Mr Bramble (he was governor of Larkmans – a nice man) in his office, and he paid for it. He wouldn't have it unloaded until he'd paid for it. Geoffrey Peacock never owed a penny.

Throughout his life Jack was always ready to help and advise:

I went home one night after sugar-beeting, and mother said someone had rung up and said he wanted to speak to me about a horse. He had got a big business and had gone into the Shire Horse job. He was going to ring at six o'clock and 'course it wasn't long before the telephone rang. It was Mr Womack. He was the old vet, a very good old boy, really old fashioned. He'd been to see these horses and told the man to ring 'that old boy who worked for Peacock's,'

He said he had got these young horses and when he walked one up and down, there was a fine water coming out of his nostrils. I said, 'Well I don't know, but always go by the opinion 'seeing is believing'. I can't do much without I see him. He said, 'Would you come and have a look?' and 'course I said I would and asked, 'Are you lit up where they are?' I said I would go at eight o'clock. I told him on the phone, 'It's likely he's got indigestion or heartburn and that the grunting is a little bit of wind. I should think he has got some bad teeth there somewhere.' I took my rasp and went there and I rasped his old teeth and got right to the back. The last one up the back you can hear by the sound of it. They don't fight much when you are doing that.

They seem to know – all of a sudden the rasp sounds different. Dip it in the pail of water and you can have another go. There is old white stuff in there and then the sound goes different, and it doesn't rasp. You go onto something flat and you can get the feeling and the sound. He had got two little bits right up the back. That was causing his indigestion. Anyway, after that he wanted me to see to the youngster he had been and bought on his own. He got him out and walked him up and down. I said, 'Well, there is one thing about it Mr A., when he was born I should think the old team-man was so disgusted he soled his arse with a big brown shovel'. That meant his arse was flat and his tail low. I said to him, 'You aren't bringing him up to win lots of championships are you, 'cos he'll never do that.' And 'course it was only his son and manager stood there with him – but I didn't know and didn't care, 'cos he asked me for my opinion and I told him didn't I? I was telling him the truth and about a year later the horse was gone.

It was not only concerns about heavy horses but people in the village would ask his advice about their ponies or horses.

People will ask you things sometimes that will put you in a muddle. I remember at Morley the new vicar moved in, and he had got two or three children. One was getting on for 14 or 15. The vicar's wife went into the shop and was talking to mother and happened to bring up they had a bit of meadow ground where they had moved into at Morley. They wanted to get a horse for them to ride – general sort of family horse. 'Course mother let it out who her husband was – which was *me*. 'Oh, I must come and see him,' and 'course that was what happened. In the finish she said she wanted a little advice about buying a horse – what sort.

Anyhow, her and the vicar came down one day and they had bought this horse. Would I have a look at it and pass my opinion? They said they had bought it off a friend of theirs. Well, a friend of theirs? They hadn't been in the parish long, so that must have been a friend of theirs wherever they came from. I didn't know, I didn't care, and well, I said I would have to see the animal.
'Yes, we will bring it down, shall we?'
So they went and got it and they got themselves rigged up. That was a laugh. They had tried to get into proper riding breeches and they were baggy and they looked a mess! They thought they were turned out top class. Anyway, she was what we call a 'flea- bitten' mare. She was getting on 'cos she weren't gone white but she was gone full of little white spots that shows a little bit of age. She was grey at one time – nice-ish sort of mare about 15 or 16 hands. I had a good look round and I couldn't find much wrong. Anyhow, I say 'Well walk her up the road and walk her back,' and I had a look. And then I say, 'Now trot her'. Well they wanted her for riding. I say, 'Trot her as quick as you can, and when you come back go right past me and back, and then trot her back again on the hard road.'

As they went past and went back again, I said, 'Well, there's one thing about it sir, she's very polite.'
He said, 'What do you mean?'
I said, 'She nods her head when she go past (that means she's a bit lame). I didn't say she was lame but I said she nod her head.
'She is very polite.' And he didn't know what I meant by that. Anyhow I said, 'Sir, if you were trying to sell this mare to me I wouldn't buy her as 100 per cent sound.' That was all I could tell them.

Anyhow Saturday morning up at Norwich as usual, at the cattle market, I was taking cattle up and as I was walking around, someone came and smacked me on the shoulder, and that was a very noted horse-dealer from out Diss way. I knew him for years. He was annoyed, and he said, 'Thank you very much Jack, you done me a good turn last week!'
I say, 'Oh yeah?'
He say, 'The people in your parish, they brought the mare back They said they wouldn't have her because Mr Juby said she was lame, but first of all they said they got it from a friend of theirs.' Well that was wrong and in my mind straight away, 'cos they had then come from somewhere away and he couldn't have been a friend to them could he? And that's when you have to be careful, when you think you are doing a good turn.

But Jack would always be careful that his 'help' did not encroach upon another man's livelihood.

But somewhere along the line I've had that way with horses and I was always ready to help somebody. If somebody wanted some help then Jack would have to go and poke his nose in! Later on in life I used to shoe people's horses sometimes. I've shod my own and I used to get a lot of respect off some of the top class blacksmiths – self taught I was. I've been at a hunt on a Boxing Day at Wymondham and there would always be somebody needing a hand. I'd have my hammer and nails and nippers and things. Someone would have got a shoe nearly off and I'd do it for them but I'd never take anything for it.

I remember once helping Michaela Weir, when I had ponies. She had been out riding her pony with Dawn Aldous and she had outgrown her pony. Her mother and father said that she had to sell her little pony if she wanted a bigger one. Well, in the end she gave in. Anyhow she had been riding the little pony that morning and she came into the yard crying
'What am I going to do Mr Juby, they aren't going to want to buy him now!'

Some interested buyers were coming to look to buy the pony that afternoon. She was upset because he had gone lame. So I say:
'Well, let's have a look at the pony.'
So I lifted his foot up to see what had happened. His shoes weren't worn up but his feet had grown over his shoes, which is a common thing that happens a lot. So I went and got my tools, took his shoe off and trimmed the surplus foot off, then tapped the shoe on again.
'Go on,' I say, 'trot it up the road, that'll be alright.'

The people come and bought the pony but as part of the deal they wanted her father, Mike, to take it and get a set of shoes on – but this is how wheels go round! He used to take horses in his trailer to a local blacksmith. Mike took his pony to be re-shod and the people were going to pick it up the next week. Well, these farriers they are a breed on their own. Anyway his blacksmith shod his pony and Mike got his trailer and paid him.
The blacksmith said. 'I've shod your pony, Mr Weir, but that will be the last time. You've had somebody else messing about with this pony.'
Mike come and told me this and I said
'I'm sorry, Mike.' I didn't want to upset him.
'I've sold that pony off,' he said, 'but I shall have to find another blacksmith to do that.'

Two nights later, Mike come up and tapped on the door:
'Jack,' he say. 'I've got news for you. I've just spoken to the blacksmith and he has just heard *you* had done the pony. He's always had great respect for you and the matter is closed. I can still go to him and he will keep doing my ponies.'

I never ever charged anybody a penny for putting their shoes on their horses or ponies because I was taking money away from the blacksmith. I have got a bottle of whisky from some people at Christmas but my principle was not to take money from another man's living.

He was always willing to help those in need it seems, however long it might take, or however it interrupted his day:

There was a man came from the other side of Watford, Mr Bowyer, he'd come to a farm sale out North Walsham way. It was one of the biggest horse sales, with a real old timer who had got harness and bridles – you name it. Everybody was going to this sale. There was an old type double furrow horse plough in the catalogue. Anyway, this man came from just off the M25 in his old type of Land Rover and he had a crippled wife with calipers on her legs, but he was determined that he was going to come and buy that plough. He'd came all that way then up Sweet Briar Road where the petrol station is and then he broke down! He had to leave the Land Rover there and get a bus, as he was determined he was going to get this plough! He left his poor wife sitting in the Land Rover until he could get back.

I was at the sale with my little old dog and my little three-penny bit lorry to see if I could buy something for my horses, and Mike Flood he come to me and asked 'Jack are you going back through Norwich?'
'Yes,' I say.
'How long are you going to be? 'Cos this gentleman wants a lift back to Sweet Briar Road.'

He'd bought the plough and his next job was to get back to his wife. She'd sat there three or four hours, poor bugger! She couldn't get out 'cos she was crippled up! He come along with me and when we got back there the poor woman was in a muddle because she couldn't get out to the toilet – she was in a state!

This was an old type of Land Rover and they'd a pipe go under the seat that had a habit of vibrating and wearing thin. Well we used to go to Reliance then for the lorries at Peacocks. They always had their lorries. So I rang them and they said, 'Jack, we can't do nothing for you, we are short handed,' and one thing and another. I tried another garage and all they could say was that they would come and get it but it would be a day or two before they could fix it.

So I rang Richard Goodings up, explained the situation and what it was. 'I know what it is,' he say, 'and I'll come out and pick it up.'

So we got his wife in my lorry and brought them home with us. Mother saw to his wife – they were both diabetics – and I took him up the farm to feed the horses. When we come home about tea-time Richard had phoned up to say the Land Rover was up there locked up and ready – £30. So then I took him to pick it up and we went back to North Walsham to get his plough. We loaded it onto the lorry, come home and stuck it onto the back of his Land Rover with the handles sticking out. They left ours at 10 o'clock at night and I say to him, 'You ring me when you get home,' and I sat up and waited until they rang up, and they thanked us ever so much. They were people we had never met before and we have been friends ever since.

It was not all hard work of course. There were plenty of fun and games. Jack was always up for a laugh and in his element when surrounded by like enthusiasts, at the shows. His watchword throughout life was to have: 'At least one really good laugh a day, however bad things are.' Dressing up was a particular delight, for example as 'Miss Juby', or a very plausible tramp:

We used to get up to all sorts of tricks at the shows. I remember at the Suffolk Show we had old L'Esperance. She was about 10 years old and she had gone almost white. They do, these Percherons – they turn white as they get older. They are black when they are born – we like to see them black. All you've got to do is look round the eyebrows and there're a couple of grey hairs here and there, and you see about two or three bits white. You know they are going to turn a grey. Well, at the show I sat there on a bale of straw having something to eat and the mare and her foal were in the horsebox. These three old ladies – quite posh – they couldn't make out why it was a white mother and a black foal. So they asked Sid, and he say,

'They belong to that man up there, you'll have to go and ask him.'

So they came and said,

'We are rather intrigued as to how the mother is white and the foal is black?'

As quick as a flash, I don't know what made me say it, I said,

'Well ma'am, I suppose there are explanations my dear. It was either a dark night or she has been with a blackman!'

Well, oh! They were disgusted but they hadn't gone ten yards afore their old heads were a-going and then they were having a real old laugh about that.

Above left: Jack loved a lark, and is here seen dressed as 'Miss Juby'.

Above: Jack dressed as a tramp.

L'Esperance was imported from France at four years old. She was over 17 hands high and weighed a ton and a quarter. She won 16 championships and was three times Royal Show Champion. She is pictured here at 10 years old.

Lime Flash Boy (father Histon Flashboy) being shown by Jack. Geoffrey Peacock (behind) with the old mare L'Esperance, bought in France. The photograph was taken at the Royal Norfolk Show (c. 1960).

Mother Willingham Daphne, father Fen Admiral and the foal Lime Kay.

When the Royal Show got to Stoneleigh, to the permanent ground then, early in the morning the head steward would come round, to see if mother was about, and have his early morning cup of tea. Old Pat Flood, a good horseman he was, he lived on his own and mother used to bake him a big loaf cake, and he used to come round there and have a cup of tea and a piece of cake. That would be his cake and he would come and have a piece every day. Mother and Mrs Hutchison – she was another 'horsey' woman – they used to go off for an hour or so to go shopping.

Much fun was had in the evenings when the show crowds had gone home – and many pranks were played! This photo was taken in the late 1950s.

At the show, after a hard day's work: from l–r: Jack, 'Tarzan' (Kenny) Mr Watling and ?

Once Mother come back with this bloody monkey and you could put your hand up him, and you could move his head. I got his tail down my back and his legs round my waist on straps and his arms around me. I went about the show ground wearing it and everybody thought it was real, even Noel Abel. He always laughs about that now.

When I got home old Jimmy Horner he came to do some shoeing. He always came home and had his dinner with us. I got this monkey out and he wholly thought it was real!

'What the hell are you going to do with that?' he say.

'I hope to get another one so I can breed them!' I say.

'You must be bloody mad Juby! Let him go,' he say.

'That I'm not!' I say, 'He'll go up that tree and we'll be all bloody afternoon trying to get him down.'

Then Ed and Shirley Dennison come one night and they were right excited to see this monkey. Ed got right riled in the end because he had brought it some monkey nuts!

And increasing age did not stop Jack's wicked sense of humour. Even later in his life, the shows still sparked off his love of 'larks':

At Peterborough show one year I had got old Duke, one of my boys, because I had at that time two Suffolks of my own, Duke and Dale. They always went as my two boys. At one end of the showground they wanted various animals and one horse from each breed – Suffolk, Shire, Percheron and Clydesdale. We were supposed to braid these horses up and show them to the public and explain anything and answer questions. Then the organiser would come about half-past ten and start explaining the animals to the public. He would say this gentleman will tell you all about Suffolks and that would last for about half an hour and then you would tie your horse up and give it some hay and relax until about two o'clock and that was what it was all about. Well anyway, I'd got old Duke. He was fat – a proper old Suffolk Punch he was, and I sat on my chair and people kept asking questions. I got fed up, so I got this piece of card and I put it up against his door and wrote on it

Braiding-up before showing one of Jack's Suffolk geldings.

'Duke, Suffolk gelding. He stands 22 hands high, he weighs two tons and something. He won the Derby in 1994 and he won the Grand National twice in 1995.'

I put that on in big black letters and people were reading that and some who knew about horses had a good laugh over it.

During the afternoon some tall man with a trilby on, along with three or four people, looked at that, stood reading the sign and then they had a little chat. He come and tapped me on the shoulder and he say to me very seriously,

'Excuse me, sir, he couldn't have won the Grand National twice in one year.'

I said, 'I beg your pardon sir, he took the bit and the jockey couldn't control him. He couldn't do nothing with him and he went round so fast the first time he couldn't stop him. He went round a second time afore he could stop him!'

He said, 'Thank you very much,' and he went off and told the others in his party! He believed it! Boy, did we have a laugh about that!

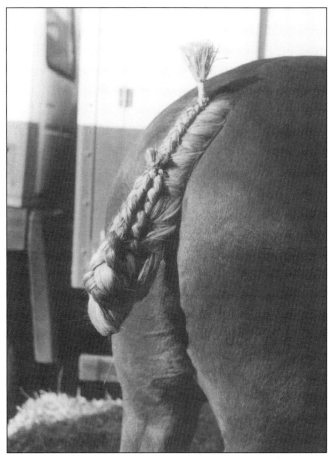

Clockwise, starting above:

Jack braiding a Suffolk Punch's tail.

The finished result! Jack was known for his expert braiding.

Jack braiding up a Suffolk Punch's mane.

Jack with Suffolk Punches in 1991.

Jack with a Suffolk colt belonging to Paul Rackham in 1991. Jack commented to the newspaper reporter. 'I have loved every minute of my life.'

Another afternoon there were crowds of people about and the man came round doing his tour and he said, 'This is Mr Juby and he will explain to you about the Suffolk horse.' This woman she stopped and asked

'How do you define the qualities of the big horse?'

Duke stood there with his back to us and he'd got an arse on him, and he was so low to the ground that made him look bigger, so I said,

'Well, first of all Ma'am, you start at the top and he has got to have the head of an angel. Then you look at the depth and he has got to have the heart of a lion ('cos you always look for a nice deep heart). When you look from the back he's got to have the backside of a farmer's daughter!' Well, that was all done in good fun.

Jack in his 70s – still game for a laugh.

What do I look for in a good heavy horse? I always work out in my mind that you want to look at your horse and picture it in a matchbox, and if his body is 100 per cent in there you are getting a line then, that's the first thing. My biggest thing is feet, I can't help it but I'm noted for it and people laugh at me. I don't care what animal it is or what colour it is, what horse it is or what breed it is, how old he is or anything – the first thing when I approach him is the feet. I look at his feet, I can't help it. It is an old saying, he must have good feet. Then you look at the conformation; the better the conformation he's got I always reckon the stronger and the longer-liver he is. That's my opinion.

People say about the head – he's got to be wide in the head to have a brain in there. Look at the horse's character. If his old head is down onto his knees he en't

too interested. He don't want to know about nothing and he hen't got no character. He wants to be upright and alert. Not too long a neck – very tapered to the
head, expanding and wide down to the shoulder. That means he'll take a good
collar and the bigger collar he have the more smaller neck he have, up at the head.
That means you can turn the collar over and put it down onto his shoulders
giving strength there in the shoulder. And short round ribs, nice round ribs – not
too many. Some of them we say he's got too many. That means he's too long in
the back. Then you go round to the back end and the tail should be all up and
not too down. If not we call them 'droop-arsed'. That means there's a weakness
in the back and a weakness in the legs. As far as I'm concerned, hocks together,
and then you get that picture in your mind.

Thorny Lady Ideal and Hempnall Annie as three and two-year olds. The horses took part in a parade through Cambridge in
September 1969, to celebrate the 50th anniversary of the introduction of the Percheron breed into this country,

Jack Juby 'Horseman Supreme', taken in January 1993, aged 72: 'Horses are individuals and you have to study each one. It's a co-operation job.'

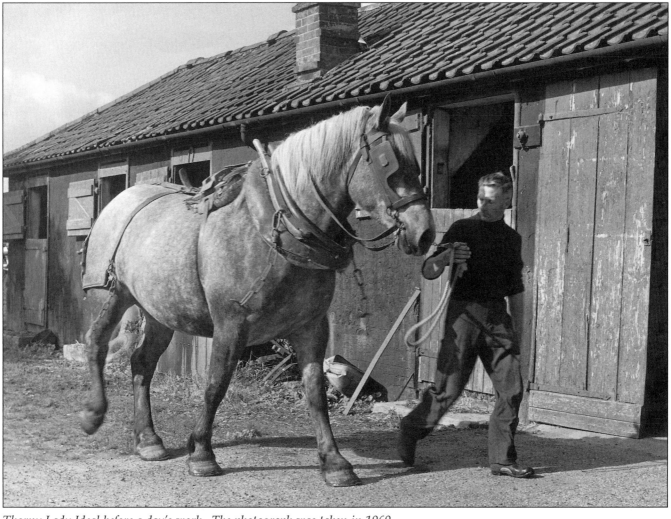

Thorny Lady Ideal before a day's work. The photograph was taken in 1969.

Jack exercising Overcoat Headline, a Percheron colt, in 1969.

Dick Jeeves Collection

Jack harrowing with horses in 1973

8

FRANCE AND BEYOND

As well as exporting horses across the world, Peacocks also introduced fresh Percheron bloodstock from France:

We used to go to France twice a year, Roger Peacock and I. He used to take me there either by boat or plane for two days, 'cos mostly with their shows they have little fairs and the main part of the town, like Wymondham, is closed. That is where they have their horses in there for a day in a sale. There is all sorts get there – and dealers. We would go to two or three of them and then we would go to a different farm, 'cos he could talk a bit of French and he had a lot of connections with their societies. That is where the Percherons came from, and all the French horses and the stallions have got a star. They are branded when they are born, so there is no fiddling their ages. They'll know in 10 years time how old that particular horse is. Anyhow, we wanted a young fresh stallion – fresh blood, 'cos if not you can get a lot of interbreeding if you don't mind. So it was a common thing to go and buy a male and then another time you want a filly or female, to come home to keep your stock a-going. And you would buy French horses – we had several away from France.

The French 'show' was not perhaps what Jack had expected.

We went to what was supposed to be their big show. Anyway, we found out where this place was and we went up an old drive. There was little old balloons as if we were going to a dance place. We got half-way up this drive and parked on this meadow place.

Charlie Saunders was with us and mother and I. Anyhow, mother and I got out and the others went round to the boot of the car and were getting their boots out, and Roger was talking in French. Well I didn't want to know all that, I wanted to get on with what I had come for. Off we go, mother and I, onto the show ground. There were cattle all tied up to trees and all the horses tied up to trees, no sheds or nothing.

There was a little old man sit there – he had got an old tammy on and he'd got an old goose sitting there next to him tied up so it shouldn't get away. And that was the show! Then we go a little bit further and some one would have a few rabbits or chickens. If you win a prize at one of their shows you get a dandy brush or a leading rein. That was really laid back! Anyhow, walking up, there was two young horses tied up to this fir tree, about 14 months old and I twigged him. Blast, I went up to him and I started measuring him for height and looking in his mouth and round his legs and looking at his feet. I liked him – there was something I liked about him.

Hotesse, an imported French filly, brought over in 1974 to improve the bloodstock.

Jack exercising a stallion in 1974.

Looking at the horse's feet with a view to buying, in France.

Jack soon became adept at what might be called 'non-verbal communication'!

Away came this old fella – a big old fella, big hands, and 'course I can't talk French. 'Non, non!' 'Course whenever I went there I always complained about the joints, 'cos the French horses hen't got no feet, 'cos they don't bother about the feet – 'cos they don't *eat* feet. That's what they breed their horses for – or 90 per cent are bred for eating, like we breed our cattle. Well, that is a recognized thing. I stood looking at this horse – talk about conformation. Anyhow, he was clean and I liked him. I pointed to the horse and tried to communicate to the old fella – 'what's this your horse?' – 'cos you can talk with your hands. We got on like a house on fire, talking with our hands. I had another look round. He knew what I meant, and he walked him back and so on. He gave him a trot and he was all right, I liked him.

A Trip to France with Roger Peacock to buy fresh stock. Jack and Margaret are to the left of the picture. Claude Bidault is third from the right and Roger Peacock fourth from the right.

Then all of a sudden we heard someone coming up – that was Roger. 'Hello Jack, you're found something you like?' Up he come and I said, 'Well, Roger that's as good a colt you'll see about here for a long while.' Anyhow he got talking to the old boy whose name was Claude Bidault and he must have had 20 of his local farmers all around, shouting and telling him what to do. Oh, that was amusing and me standing there like a fool had no idea what they were all on about. Anyhow, Roger came back and said, 'You like him Jack?'

I said, 'He's alright, he's sound.'

The inevitable meal was quite an affair, with wine playing a prominent part, even if Jack began to suspect his judgement was being deliberately clouded.

We had a look at one or two more and anyhow we finished up in a big old tin hut for a meal. Well, in France a meal is a meal, you can say what you like, wherever you are. Food! I never knew anything like it. There were two rows of tables and long forms you sat on. We got there at about 1 p.m. and sat down to the meal. Every course there was a bottle of wine – more and more wine. Then all of a sudden, the Lord Mayor get up and proposed a toast to our English friends and we all had to get up. And then you would have another plate of food. Then the head of the Percheron Society would get up and he would make a little speech and then he would propose a toast to our English friends – and there would be another glass-full, and that went on till 4 p.m. The food was magnificent but half way through the meal somebody in our party (and that wasn't me, it wasn't mother and it wasn't Charlie Saunders) went arse-over-head onto the floor, and he was out. They tried to get him up but he was out of it.

A young lady sat dead opposite me and the old man that owned the horse sat two down from me. Well that was niece and uncle, and she could speak English. She said, 'Have you bought the horse yet? Uncle wants to know have you bought the horse yet?' So I said, 'No, No.'
She said, 'Why? – too much money?' And I signalled he would have to come down. Then they had a little chat – I twigged this. After a minute or two she picked up the bottle of wine and topped my glass up. This happened two or three times. I could see the message he was giving to her to fill my glass up, and I put my hand over the glass and said 'No, No, you fill uncle's up again.' And he and I looked at each other and he could see the funny side of that. And do you know what, he and I were friends for years, and he used to send me bottles of Calvados, and he came over one year and had a day out with me in the lorry. We had a good day out and neither of us could speak each other's language. He was a good old boy.

Margaret was doing her bit for Anglo-French relations by getting to know the town's chief of police!

At six o'clock, they had to help all of us, except mother. That was the day when mother got in with the head of the police. She got on the top table and they sat there arm in arm and they sat having a drink with their English friend. Mother was taller than him. Do you know, we weren't safe to be left on our own! We had a police car in front and one behind to take us through the town to our hotel.

That is when we bought Mistero. We had him home and brought him up and he won for three or four year, and then Roger sold him to go to Australia and I took him down to Kent for him to go into quarantine for three weeks. They get all the horses together, then they all go on a plane together and transport them to where they have to go to. He was nine-year old when we sold him and 10-year old when he finally got there. He had six weeks travelling when he landed to go across Australia. That was just before Christmas, and they are a year older on January 1. I sent them a photograph and told them all about him, and Roger had a photograph come, and he'd gone completely white. They had got him in harness, pulling trees out of a plantation.

Peacocks exported a lot of horses over the years: Africa, Australia, Canada, New Zealand, Kenya and Pakistan. There was a write-up in the papers about Mistero. He was one of the first heavy horses used for artificial insemination. He was a big horse and he left foals out in Kenya.

We have got friends in Australia – Mr and Mrs Parkes. They came and bought horses off us twice, and the second time they come they bought Histon Highlight, about four years old – the one I took to Windsor in front of the Queen. They bought him under one condition – that I went with him! Anyhow, eight o'clock that morning, walking round the stables at the farm and saying our goodbyes, Mr Parkes said to me, 'Now you will bring your wife and come and stay with us'. And I said, tapping my pocket, 'Well, hopefully I will when I get enough in here.' He said, 'Oh, don't worry about that, your fares will be paid for and you will have the time of your lives.' I should have took him up on that. They wanted the horses for riding and herding the cattle up. He was a fairly smallish horse – about 16.1 – and agile. Good for what they wanted – big and strong.

Even if Jack was unable to get as far as Australia, he did enjoy one brief holiday, with Margaret, to the Isle of Wight:

That was where mother and I later on had our one and only holiday on the Isle of Wight, the only holiday we ever had. Mrs Ruthven – who mother used to work for at the shop and post office, at Morley – they took mother there. The Ruthvens used to go every year because they had a caravan there. They had the same one every year, and because Mr Ruthven had died, we had the option to go with her for a fortnight. We took separate cars because I knew I couldn't stop a fortnight. So on the Sunday I left mother there and come home. I had had my week, and that was enough.

Jack and Margaret at Mrs Ruthven's caravan site on the Isle of Wight. Jane Ruthven, her daughter, is with them.

And Jack received an amazing welcome home from his animal friends:

When I got home and I turned in from Attleborough and come down by Paterson's corner, as I come down to 'The Laurels' I saw the stallion up at the farm. I went indoors and was just making a cup of tea and I nearly jumped out of my skin when the telephone rang. It had been put in when we were away! It was Mrs Peacock and she said, 'You're home then, you've been home nearly 20 minutes haven't you?'
I say, 'Yeah.'
'We knew,' she say, 'we knew because that stallion has been shrieking his head off and the mares up on the meadow they are calling! I ran indoors and said to mother, 'Jack is home, I bet he's home and that's when I called you.'
I'd been away a week and they knew I was home. As I turned into Waterloo Farm, Mrs Peacock came out and said:
'For goodness sake go and see to Fen Admiral. We have been worried about him all week, he hasn't eaten anything.'
My bales of hay still laid there. I went up to him and patted him
on his neck. I gave him his usual mint and said:
'You silly old bugger you.' He turned round and started tucking into his hay. Mrs Peacock couldn't believe it.

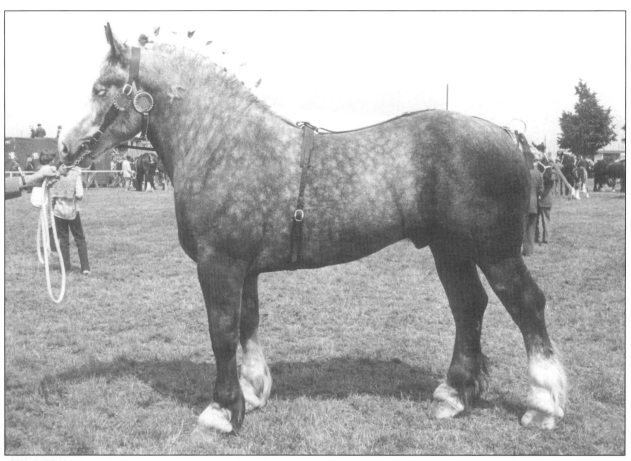

Mistero, bought in France, at about 14 months old.

Jack with Mistero in 1982, walking around the farm.

Exercising Fen Admiral, Jack's stallion friend who called out to welcome him back from holiday. The background is Lime Tree Farm.

Another remarkable moment, with a quite different breed of horse, was recalled by Mrs Peacock's late husband Roger, in a newspaper interview:
'Jack was given a hackney colt, wild, high-spirited, un-handled by man. Next day, Jack had walked up and put a halter on. I'd never seen anything like it! I don't think there's another man in England who could have done that in 24 hours.'

Roger Peacock's stable at Morley in 1975, with his Suffolk filly Rowhedge Meg on the right, bought for showing purposes. Percheron filly Lime Janet is in the centre. They are being admired by Fen Admiral, the Percheron stallion, on the left.

Jack puts the 'supreme champion' rosette on Lime Claude at the 1989 Royal Norfolk Show.

Lime Claude going for a run, with Lime Tree Farm in the background.

Lime Claude presents a cheque for £400 to Quidenham Hospice in 1992! Molasses was put on the practice cheque to make him hold it!

Lime Claude at the Kimberley Show in 1991.

Lime Claude at Kimberley Stallion Parade in 1991. Twenty two stallions paraded on that occasion.

Turning the tables! Jack caught Dick Jeeves, the EDP photographer, holding Lime Claude.

Dick Jeeves Collection

9

THE STORY OF A FOAL

During the time Jack was working for Geoffrey Peacock he recalls the story of one particular foal:

A filly foal was born one morning in the stable and the governor he came down at about eight o'clock time: 'What's happened – oh, a filly foal. Everything alright?' 'Yeah,' I replied. Anyway, we had to decide what to call her. We had to name them straight away for registration and one thing and another, and 'cos that was Lime Tree Farm everything was Lime something, and he say, 'Jack that come out of Lime so and so and that come out of Lime so and so. He went back to seven generations and I had foaled them all, down in that same stable over a period of time. Generally speaking they are four-year old before they have a foal. When you think about it that is fantastic.

Well anyway, talking about this foal, I had just come back previously from the marshes. I'd got back three young mares – they had been 'rented out' – what we call rented out on the marshes – and brought them home to the farm. I put them down on the meadow at Meadowland Cottage where the Wortleys lived – because we lived up at 'The Laurels' then. One of them had got damaged feet, so I had to give her some attention two or three times.

I woke up one morning with the telephone ringing. A voice said 'It's Lucy.' It was Lucy Wortley, but 'cos my mare was called 'Lime Lucy', I was getting confused. It was a crispish sort of morning so I tore off up there. The mare was foaling – a fortnight early – and the others were getting excited and jamming round her. She had a beautiful filly foal but one of the others jammed over top of it and broke its thigh. We got the vet out – our vet Tom Muir being on holiday, he had got a temporary vet in. This young lady vet come down all dressed in white and one thing and another. So I got two chaps away from the farm, young Ray and someone, and they brought a tractor and trailer with some bales of straw and backed the trailer into a low hole on the meadow and there were three or four of us man-handled it onto the back of the trailer. I sit on top of the trailer and led the mare behind and went across the fields. Mother and them all thought it looked like a funeral procession!

We went back up to the farm, to the old stable yard. There was a big step into the stable so that meant the trailer kept level. I tied the mare up and give her some food, and we lifted the foal off. In the meantime the vets had been called from McLintocks in Norwich. McLintock, the head vet, he come over and had an examination. He brought X-ray plates and we struggled and took X-rays of it. Mother came down and it was handy then because she had been working at the Wayland Hospital, and she give a hand. McLintock took the plates back to Norwich to be examined – and 'course I didn't understand things then – but he brought the plates back and said she had a compound fracture. He shew me the plates and it looked like old saw teeth, all jagged.

'Cos this had been going on for two or three hours and the foal had been getting out of position by then, we had to get a little pulley rigged up to the big stable door post and another round the top of the foal's leg and another rope rounds its leg to another pulley. We had to keep stretching and stretching and the vet gradually felt and felt all them little teeth went in together. Amazing you know, amazing! We got it done and Mother helped. They had to make pail-fulls of plaster of Paris – if you imagine the size of its leg and it had to be done top to bottom to the ankle. And 'cos that laid there (and 'cos people they don't understand), 'cos that laid there the poor mother – her first foal tied up over there – she was getting anxious. Milk was running out of her. You could see her thinking – what is happening to my baby?

Getting the young foal on its feet, one leg encased in plaster of Paris , was a challenge – and one left to Jack's uncanny empathy with the way a horse functioned:

And 'cos that had laid there so long – and a horse you see, how do a horse get up? It get up front feet first and that couldn't manage that leg could it? The back end was hopeless and Mr McLintock and young Ray tried. Then Mr McLintock he say to the others, 'Just come out of the way and leave Jack alone. He'll do something. 'Course the natural thing for them to do is pull their front feet right out and the head comes out on the front feet. Then they jump and push themselves up, and 'course this foal couldn't do that could it, the back leg was heavy. So I had to get its head and neck and feet in the right position. Twice I had to do that and I got its dock and my hand into its bum and the other one into its flank and pushed it up onto its front feet. Oh, marvellous! That was like pushing a wheelbarrow up, and I gradually pushed that and got it over to her mother. It went straight to her mother with its head up underneath, and started sucking at the mother. Cor! What an achievement!

Jack needed to sleep close to the young foal, and had to buy an old caravan to use:

I went to Lowestoft in a hurry, and Ivan Cooke rang up again and we had been talking, and he told me where there was a cheap little old caravan – a little one-berth caravan in good condition. Then mother and I we had to empty the purse, and we bought this tiny little old caravan, 'cos I didn't live at the farm. So I went and got that and set that up in the corner near the stable door and ran the electric there and that is where I lived for three weeks. That had got to be fed every two and a half hours and 'cos it couldn't get up to help itself, that had to be lifted up and took to its mother. And when it had finished it had to be taken to lay out of her way, in case she knocked the foal over, because she was a young mare. I laid that up there against the wall and that is where it had got to lay until Jack went back to feed it – and that was every three hours or so. That meant that I couldn't go home. Well, I went home to wash and eat and drink. Mr McLintock, he gave me his private number and he say: 'Any query Jack, ring me and I will be out as soon as I can.'

It was getting on ever so well, getting up and sucking, but 'cos it was laying there doing nothing, and 'cos it was growing and getting fat, it was getting a big thing to keep pulling about. And 'cos I was taking sugar beet into the factory and I could do Bury in two – two and a half hours, then I would pick the foal up, leave that sucking while I loaded the beet up, run across the farm and go back and lay it down again. I'd go home and have a cup of tea and take another load of beet in and get back in time to put the foal to the mare again. Cor, that got cold at night!

But Jack's instinct was that something was wrong, even if at first he could not work out what was happening:

And 'cos that went on for six weeks and in the course of that six weeks, if you want to know the history, I went home worried out of my mind. Mother said, 'Whatever is the matter with you?' I say, 'My foal, there's something amiss and I didn't know what.' And 'cos it was plastered all the way down its leg and a filly foal being a female foal, when it wetted that had wetted inside the plaster, because that would wee itself different to a colt foal. And it had wet and it had gone down into its hock and the plaster had gone all pappy inside there. I took the bull by the horns and rang Mr McLintock and out he come and we had to get mother out there again and young Ray. It was a long while and they had to chip all that plaster off and that had all gone funny in there. So what do we do? Now I kept sitting at the head watching, 'cos it was a mask then, not a needle. I kept checking and the eyes were alright. I remembered going to school with a young boy, Billy Abel, and he had a leg-iron – the old fashioned sort – because he suffered from polio.

Well I got young Ray – he was a handy young kiddie on the farm – with his welding set, and one thing and another, and he made me a set of calipers and I've still got a set somewhere. 'Course he had to joint everywhere didn't he – the knee joint etc, and got down to the ankle. But we had to leave the foot free and we had to join the foot cage with some wires that were expandable, so we could alter the screw one way. We could alter it half an inch at a time, 'cos she kept growing every day didn't she. *What* a success! We had photographers taking photos of it and it was a great success that went on.

But they were still not free of problems, and this time the calipers were to blame:

McLintocks said it would be 10 to 12 weeks. It got to the six weeks and I had trouble again. I woke up one morning to go into the stable and there laid the foal and it had got the other bloody leg inside the caliper! Well, how do you get out of that – me on my own! Jack got out of it somehow, but there was still something wrong. We got McLintock out again and of course when we came to realize, that foal had grown three and half inches but the caliper hadn't. That was cramping it.

Jack had sacrificed his own comfort and time, sleeping in a cold caravan, with a 40 watt bulb for light, for the whole 12 weeks that he was looking after this young foal:

While I was looking after the foal, I was sleeping one night in the caravan and I used to run a 40-watt bulb from the stable in the top of my caravan, and that just kept the frost off the window – just a little bit of comfort, and 'course as soon as I woke up I got a little bit of light.

I was doing everything free. I didn't get a penny for what I'd done. You don't hear of them sort of things nowadays. But it had its compensations, didn't it? Money isn't everything is it? And that foal was Lime Josephine. But I wouldn't do it again and I wouldn't advocate anyone to do it. The misery and the worry – oh the worry! She lived to be 12-year old, but I don't know who else would have persevered so long. And all the foals I have had over the years, and if I can say it without bragging or anything, I was renowned for my midwifery. I used to go round all over the place, foaling people's mares down who didn't know what they were doing, and all that kind of thing. If they were worried, they'd get Jack to go and sit up with them.

And Jack explained how he trained the young foals:

Every foal I had on the farm at about three days old I'd get them out – out onto the pasture. I'd always lead the mare out and it would be strange for the foal and you didn't know what it was going to do, whether it was going to follow mummy properly or whether it was going to go back and get lost and that sort of thing. Take your time and get it out onto the pasture and hold the mare there and don't let her go galloping off. Let the foal get its bearings and they all go through identical procedure year in and year out. They will go round and think, 'Cor, this is lovely.' They run round in a little circle round mother, then they'd get frightened, whinnie and then come back to mother. After a minute they go in another little circle and they'd get a little further round and a little braver. And 'course two or three time like that, then you could take the halter off and let them go, but this foal I have been talking about, 'course that couldn't go where it wanted to, could it?

Jack's sheer affection for these animals comes through in his description of what followed:

Young Jonathan from Cornwall was staying with me to learn about horses. So I go back after breakfast and I say, 'Jonathan, we're going to get the foal out this morning. It's still in its iron leg.' Jonathan led the mare out and the foal kept coming out, one step at time, and I kept pushing it and pushing it. Then I stood there holding the mare and I cried (I cry more when I talk about it). The little foal it stood there and she was in this lovely world. The sun was shining and all of a sudden she wanted to do what every foal I'd ever had wants. She wanted to gallop off, and she couldn't, could she. So the little bugger stood and galloped on her two front feet. Well, if that wouldn't bring tears to anybody's eyes I don't know what will, but you see that was nature wasn't it. But there you are, she came good in the end and that made it all worth while.

Jack had had a close involvement with Mr McLintock over the whole period of the foal's story, and it was only right that he should see the results of their joint work:

After a period of time I had got to take three young mares down to the marsh again, right early in the spring time, take them down there and turn them off for the summer. I rang McLintock up (he had retired) on his home number and found out where he lived. I put the horse on the back of the lorry and at eight o'clock I was outside his house and I unloaded her in his garden. Cor, weren't he pleased. He phoned his daughters up to come and take photos of it. Well, it was his accomplishment, weren't it?

We got out of that and it lived, and from three year old it bred two or three foals and the only mark you could see was a white mark where the irons had been round.

PONIES AND GYMKHANAS

The size of the horse did not matter to Jack, and later in life he developed an enthusiasm for the lightweight horse scene:

It was Alison the middle daughter, she was the only one that had any inclination with the horses. She envied the other kids going out with their ponies and that, 'cos we hadn't got any money to buy ponies with in them days. Anyhow there used to be a regular Tombland Easter Fair up at Norwich with a pony sale. 'Course Jack had to go there and have a couple of hours off, and I left home – Meadowland Cottage – that morning and 'course Alison, she said, 'Dad, you always promised me a pony. You're going to buy me one today,' and that is when I bought the pony we called Morley Surprise.

Alison Downes, Jack's daughter, at the Aylsham Show in 1965 with Morley Surprise.

I got to Tombland Fair and there was this poor little old pony. Roger Peacock he was a lad home from school. He used to go to market and buy half a dozen old sheep and bring them home and try and earn a pound or two, and that was how he started. He was up at Tombland Fair and I wanted to buy this pony and I hadn't got enough money. Well, the situation was that when Roger bought anything and wanted them moved – a few sheep from market perhaps – his father would let me take the farm lorry and do the carting for Roger, but Roger had to pay me my time – the old man wouldn't pay me for my time. He used to say to me, 'It's up to the boy, he'll have to pay your time Jack.'

I was looking at this here pony and I told Roger about it and he said, 'Well, I'll buy that for you.' I always remember we got a bit of chalk and we pencilled on the post in the cattle yard. There was my time to come too, and we reckoned that all up and that came to 32 pound, and that is what he bought the pony for. So that squared his bill up and I didn't have to part with any money and that's how we got the pony home.

But when the likelihood of a good offer came, the pony had to be sold:

Jack's daughter Mavis (right) and her friend Gillian Tooke, at the 1965 Aylsham Show. The goat was called Skippy.

We used to take it out and feed it on the side of the road. I wormed him and done his teeth and he got a good pony. We took him to the Aylsham Show in 1965 and different places. Then Alison got so she could ride and do, and play about with him. Geoffrey Peacock came to see me one day and he say, 'You've got a good pony here now Jack. He's quiet and all right. I got someone who wants to buy that.' It was someone from Attleborough. Peacocks had sold him a little grey pony two or three years previous and they had outgrown it and they wanted a bigger one. After a lot of heartbreak they came round and tried the pony out and I sold the pony for a hundred pounds and I had got to deliver it. I was going to Diss the Monday morning with the lorry with two horses on and I put the pony on the back and called on the way to Diss. I unloaded the pony and the lady took me indoors and opened the cheque book and said, 'Who do I make the cheque out to – Mr Peacock?' I say, 'You make that out to me, it's my pony'. She writ me a cheque for a hundred pound and 'cos that was a lot of money then and 'cos there were a lot of tears, I say to Alison, 'I promise I will buy you another one.'

And soon another pony materialised for his daughter:

Well I goes over to Willingham in the lorry with the wife and children one day to see the Garner family and have a cup of tea. We did this perhaps twice a year, and he took me to what I called the Fens. There was this little Welsh pony right down the bottom meadow and he didn't know she had then foaled and that she had got this little foal. It was no bigger than a hare. You could have picked it up and carried it and I bought it down there but it had got to stay until it was weaned. I paid £60 for it and 'course he turned out to be Simon. The first cheque I ever wrote out in my cheque book was £60 for Simon. We had never had a cheque book until then. I can remember when I first got that book we stood there like a couple of fools. We didn't know how to write out a cheque. It is laughable today.

Jack having a laugh, on his pony Simon.

We got him going, jumping and so on. He would do anything you ask. He was a clever little old bugger, too clever at times, and Peacock he came to me one Saturday and he say some friends of his had bought their kids a pony and they wanted to get it to gymkhanas. I didn't know nothing about gymkhanas, not in them days, but they had got no transport for their pony and they couldn't load it. They should have gone somewhere the week before but they couldn't load it, so he say, 'You can load anything, so I have told them I will get you to go and see to it the week-end'.

The world of gymkhanas was new to Jack, but as usual he threw himself into it whole-heartedly:

So I took his lorry on the Sunday and met over on Cringleford Green. The whole family were there – mother, father, aunty, uncle – the lot were there, and their pony. I had got my little pony on there 'cos I thought if I take him he would load on the lorry anytime. So I thought, I'll take him and he would encourage the other one if there was any bother. So that's what we done. We got down to Horsford, down Sandy Lane, and I got a gal onto Simon – and go to hell if she didn't go and win a rosette time I was waiting for these other people. So that was the first winning rosette with Simon.

Well, then it was, 'What are we going to do next Sunday' – and the next Sunday, and 'course that started the ball rolling. And then 'course I had to start to beg and borrow a lorry – usually from the farm – but that was always a wheel within a wheel – I'll scratch your back and you scratch mine, so to speak. I mean by that, that regular on a Saturday morning I'd take something up to the sale at Norwich, mostly cattle. That would mean leaving the lorry there from 10 o'clock Saturday all day waiting in case he had bought anything. So he would take a chance on that and he would send me home again. So then I'd get a phone call: 'I've bought some cattle, can you come and pick them up?' I didn't used to charge him nothing for that so that meant I could borrow the lorry on a Sunday. It was the same old thing – nobody parted with any money.

'Course then, with the little pony we won and won, no matter where we went with that pony. He was a little character. Could that horse jump! Firstly we started off with my young nephew Roger jumping him, and then they got one of their own, and then that meant I had to find a rider for my pony and that was when Dawn Seville came on the scene – a little girl about 11 years old, and she was just right for him. She lived in Wicklewood and she was pony-minded and that. She had been sent to Mulbarton to have riding lessons (unbeknown to me). I didn't know the people and she come down and looked and said, 'Can I have a ride, Mr Juby, can I have a ride on your pony?' And so that was how they clicked and that is how we started to go to gymkhanas. Then 'cos after two years or so she had outgrown the little 12.2-hand Simon, so 'course I then had to find another rider. That was when Paul Whiterod came along. Eight-year-old – and he could ride! He had got a pony of his own and weren't getting on too well with it. I popped him onto Simon and away they went. But of course that meant I had got a good rider with no pony. That finished up that I got Crusader, and he turned out very, very well, and he was the right size to see Dawn through, and boy, could he jump? And they clicked.

Paul Whiterod and Dawn Aldous in 1973 with Simon and the rosettes and trophies he had won.

Soon Jack and his young riders were moving up the competition ladder. And Crusader did well, despite his unfortunate start in life.

Then of course the ponies had to be affiliated and you went up a step from the gymkhanas with rules and regulations which I knew nothing about, but we soon fell into that. Crusader went up the Norfolk Showground and had we continued with him I'm sure the horse could have gone through to the Royal Show and eventually onto Wembley. But Dawn was at work by then and I just couldn't afford it, but I think if he had been in other hands he would have made it. He could have gone farther than he did. I got a good offer for him once. He did a lot of jumping. The horse loved his jumping. People used to say – even judges – 'Don't your horse love his jumping.' He never used to get flustered, or worried. He come out of a Percheron mare by Vorolla. That mare we took to that stallion five times. Crusader was the last one and he was the smallest one of the bunch and he weren't too good a prospect looking at him, 'cos he turned out to be a rig (which means when he turned 14 or 15 months old he had only one testicle). You get that now and again, and my theory is that it always does affect the brain.

That Saturday morning the vets were coming to do two Percheron colts so I took Crusader down the yard with them to be done. And 'cos when the vet come he said he would have to take a chance because he had only got one testicle, and you aren't supposed to do that, you see. Because later on you could have trouble, and I remember later on when he was down on the marshes with the other horses, the marsh man said, 'You'll have to come and get him, Jack,' because he was playing the other horses up. In his mind he was still a stallion, you see. In the finish I had to go and get him, 'cos he belonged to Roger. Then he say, 'That's no good Jack, he'll never be any good. You'll have to take him and have him put down.'

Anyhow, I got him in that yard. His little old feet they were so untidy, but I couldn't take a horse with feet like that – it was bad for my reputation! So I went down the yard there and trimmed his feet up. Pulling about him I got his front foot up between my leg and I had a breather. And then I put my hand up underneath where his pouch was and I pressed it and poked it and kept pressing, and I found all of a sudden one dropped. It dropped in like a hen's egg and dropped into my hand and that was the other testicle – it had come down. Roger came into the yard and I said to him, 'You needn't worry about taking him to Pilgrim's (the slaughterer). You want to phone Muir the vet up and get him to come up and take the other testicle away.' Muir came and took the other testicle away but 'course that then went wrong and he bled and bled and we couldn't stop the bleeding. Roger said, 'We ought to have taken him to Pilgrim in the first place. 'Well,' I said to him, 'I'll tell you what I'll do. I'll take a chance on him.' and I give about £50 or £60 for him. I took him home across the fields. It took a long while to get him right and 'course he turned out to be Laurel Crusader, a bigger horse and the right horse for Dawn to ride.

Simon was still being ridden, and I used to take sometimes four various ponies, picking the youngsters up as I went through the villages to go to gymkhanas. Laurel Crusader he come good in the finish and he come there and he jumped until he was 27 years old, unbeaten everywhere he went. It was a well-recog-

Jack on Crusader.

nized thing. I went to Dereham to the riding school at Westfield. I went there one night, and I said to Mr Guest – I shall never forget it – I said to him, 'The next time I come, I shall leave the old hoss at home.' He said, 'Why?' I say, 'It must be heartbreaking for these others to see me unload him and they know bloody well when they see him come here they aren't going to win'. But anyhow, he put me wise. He say, 'Don't do that Jack,' he say, 'whatever you do, don't do that. That's what they all keep coming for – to see if they can beat him!' So he had got a point hadn't he? He was a fantastic horse.

And Simon was also fantastic, so much so that Jack turned down what must have been a small fortune at that time, from someone who wanted to buy the pony:

Simon he was another. I shall never forget Alan Oliver. He was a top class show jumper in them days. He offered me a lot of money for him – £1,000 – and he cost me £60. I took him to Watton show-ground on the Wednesday. 'Course Dawn had to have the day off school so she could show him off jumping. She just put him over a couple of little jumps and Alan Oliver offered me £1,000, all in notes. And I hadn't got a ha'penny 'til pay-day. But I wouldn't take it.

Two weeks later, mother she came up the meadow where I was with the ponies and she say, 'Telephone for you, it's a man from London.' It was a Sunday morning. It was Alan Oliver phoning from Windsor, ('course he used to look after the Queen's children's ponies and that sort of thing). He say, 'Have you sold that yet?' I say, 'No'. So he say, 'Well, how much do you want for the bloody pony?' But of course I said 'no'. Mother, bless her old heart, she say, 'Father, what are you thinking of, turning down all that money!' But money couldn't buy all the pleasure he was to give us over the next 20 years. He was such a character, and really I was fortunate enough to have two.

Crusader was taken everywhere and knew exactly how to deal with riding against the clock. And Jack paid tribute to the camaraderie of the other competitors, who seemed equally pleased to share in the horse's success:

Old Crusader he went everywhere winter or summer doing his jumping. Loved it he did. He got crafty though, and the last 10 years of his life, crafty old bugger, (everybody will tell you) he knew when he was against the clock. He wouldn't get excited. Cool as a cucumber he was. We went to Lopham and the big boys used to come down there warming up their horses in the arena. They used to sweat, but I used to say to Dawn, 'Do a couple of jumps to warm him up,' and that was his lot.

Well, one day there were eight in the jump-off. I went in there and see one or two of the others going against the clock. I used to give Dawn the down whether to go against the clock and go for it, or go for a place. She was lucky this time, she was the last to go, and this is where it is so nice amongst the horse fraternity. There were eight competitors against me and they had been there all day. We got into the grand finale and they say, 'What's he going to do, Jack?' and I told Dawn 'I don't know what to tell you to do.' And the door opened and the dong went and along came Crusader – over this one and over that one and we all stood there silent and I shall never forget it. 'Oh God', he come out and he hadn't touched a pole Then they gave out over the tannoy, 'Well, that clever old bugger, he's done it again – he beat the clock.' My seven competitors all went mad. They all jumped up and down and clapped. Now weren't that nice. Then they all come into the ring and away come Crusader to get his rosette – his old head on one side and his old tail a-going – to go and line up in front of the judge to get their rosettes. And Mrs Attenborough give out over the tannoy, 'Surely this grand old gentleman must go down as the Milton of East Anglia.' He had won yet again.

Jack's instinct about horses had proved so right again. Riders transfer their anxieties to their horses, and over-practising before the events can cause these anxieties.

Dawn Aldous with Crusader and the rosettes he won.

I've seen these people with bloody good horses out there putting them over the practice jumps. They would be sweated up before they went into the ring. See, I would never allow that. I used to say, 'Just put him over them twice, Dawn, that's enough.' He never did need it and that way he never got worried, and what I am trying to stress is, the excitement goes through the horse. I cannot impress enough on people that the leading rein, or whatever you have, is like electric going straight through to the horse. If *you* have got any qualms, it will upset the horse immediately. You have got to be so full of confidence and that will transfer to the horse – just like that.

And Jack gave an example of what he meant:

The biggest event in our little way was to qualify for the Royal Norfolk Show, to have our horse jumping. I was already up at the show with the heavies and Dawn came along that morning to put Crusader in there, with a bit of hay and one thing and another. That afternoon Dawn went and put her name down on the board. Anyhow 10 minutes to two (she had got to be in there at two) I said, 'Come on gal, let's get him out and give him a round.' When I put her up onto his back and give her a leg up and get her foot into the stirrups, that was when Dawn's legs were gone. And by the time they had got round the boxes, old Crusader lifted his tail and the shit just flew out of him.

That had then got through to him just like that, and I knew then that weren't going to do any good. I went up to Dawn and said, 'Now do you want me to withdraw him? I'll be the one to withdraw him, so there is no reflection on you.' But she insisted on going in, and she did her round with faults, but the point I am trying to make here is, he was the most placid old animal in England but that got through to him and nine times out of ten it is not the animal's fault, it is transferred by the rider or handler. Once the confidence has gone, you are in trouble.

Billy Bumfrey, working with his two Shires. Billy was a friend and horseman much respected by Jack.

Jack remembered his old friend Billy Bumfrey, as 'one of the best horsemen I ever knew.'

Talking about the light-weight horses and ponies I used to keep for my own personal pleasure, I had this old mare. How that came about was through Billy Bumfrey, an old mate of mine. It was Billy that introduced me to my old mare that I had, to breed lightweights from. We were at the Spring Heavy Horse Show at Peterborough one bitterly cold day. We stood talking there and during the conversation he mentioned about Mrs Knights. She had been to Newmarket and bought this two-year- old young filly. She wanted something to go hunting with. Well, she had the horse a year but it turned out to be a bastard. It had been too highly bred, that was the trouble. I used to go over and see Billy some Sunday afternoons. I used to go down to the farm with him because he had got something to go down there for. Anyhow, we went down there this particular Sunday afternoon: 'What you've got out there on that paddock, Billy?' I say.

The mare was out on the paddock with some donkeys and 'course I was over the gate and went to have a look at her. He says, 'You don't want to go over there Jack, you stay this side. She's a bugger, Jack. I don't know what they are going to do with her. She's a wrong 'un. She's not right up here.'

Anyhow, talking to him at the Peterborough Horse Show, he say,

'I don't know Jack, I think I've got you lumbered!'

I say. 'What!'

He said, 'We've had a meeting with Madam about the filly, and I told her there's only one man I know will be able to do anything with her and that was you, and she is going to contact you.'

Jack with the mare Laurel Crown Court, bought via his friend Billy Bumfrey from Mrs Knights. Eight or nine foals were bred from her.

Well, she did and wanted me to go over and view the horse. She wanted two or three thousand pound for her. I hadn't got that in pennies let alone in pounds! We were talking and I said,

'Do you realise madam, it will take at least 12 months to get her quiet enough for my daughter to ride? She'll come to it, but there will be a lot of hard work involved.'

Her husband came up and parked his Rolls Royce. He'd just come back from London. He stood behind and she turned round to him and said,

'Regardless of the money, I think he is the man that ought to have her.'

So I bought her for £200, and she was a top class horse. Her grandfather was Escalon – as well known as Red Rum in his hey-day. I always maintained in my lifetime, you can get a four year old champion stallion and you can get a four year old champion mare, but that don't mean that you are going to breed a champion out of them! I've always gone back in my mind and picture the grandparents on both sides. That work out on a good average – go back to grandparents. I bred eight or nine good foals from her.

Four month old Laurel Cavalier, at the Wayland Show.

Jack's mare bought through Billy Bumfrey with a foal shown at the Watton Show.

Jack particularly remembers his old friend Billy's funeral.

We met while I worked at Knights of Stody and lived at Edgefield. He was a good horseman, a real top class horseman. He used to be at Stody as head groom, not at the Stud but on the farms, and he used to have young horses and break them in. He was a top class ploughman and won a lot of ploughing matches in his time. He always turned his horses out well, clean bridle, black harness and the brasses shone – that was a picture. At one time he was a Shire man. The farm he was bred and born on were Shire people for years and years. When old Rix died that automatically went into the estate, so Billy finished up working for the estate – so he had to go into Suffolks then. Blast, couldn't he plait a horse up and turn it out. I took a Shire to his funeral – that was my wish 'cos I knew Billy would have wanted it. David Banham's Rory – jet black that was, with the white feet and fetlocks and a white face. I done him up with heavy white wool mane and tail and I took him there. But he hadn't been out – he hadn't seen nothing like that. We pulled up on the road outside the crematorium, unloaded him off the lorry and away come the procession with the hearse. It was a woman funeral director from Holt.
She said, 'You lead.'
I thought I was going to follow behind! I took him through those gates and up that drive. There was an old man in the bushes cutting the grass with a lawn-mower. He'd been doing something with that and he had been revving that up, and that was a smoking and going and I thought, blast he's going to jump when I go past that – he must jump! He didn't though, he walked at the right pace. I didn't lead him – he walked. There's a big glass dome thing there and I thought I was going to part with the hearse and that was going to go under the dome, but the funeral director waved me under there as well. His feet echoed and I was amazed. The horse was in a daze. David he come and took over – 'cos he stood outside – and led him back so I could go to the funeral service. He hadn't got 20 yards down the road when he bucked and kicked – I thought David was going to lose him! Nobody can explain, and I was on tenterhooks. A young horse like that, never been out much, but he was calm, and when we stood waiting to go under the dome thing he stood with his nose on top of the flowers on top of the hearse. I didn't have to touch him. This 'affinity with the horse,' Keith Skipper called it. I can't explain it.

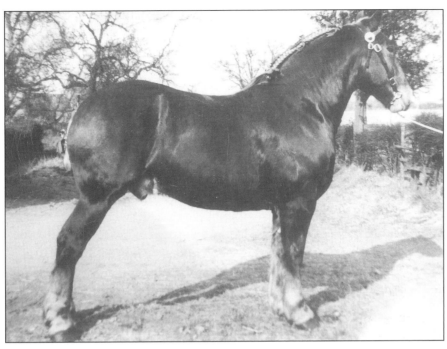

Stallion (probably Captain).

Rory at Billy Bumfrey's funeral, June 1990.

EPILOGUE
BY ALISON DOWNES

Unfortunately, the tapes stopped here, and this was when Jack was still talking about doing gymkhanas, with Simon and Crusader. Jack became too ill to tape any more of his life, so hopefully I can bring the story up to date. My deepest regret, of course, was the fact that I didn't do these tapes 10 years earlier, before his illness took hold. There was so much more that could have been said, and perhaps only the tip of the iceberg was achieved. But in saying that, we have still captured a rich and rewarding life full of his love for horses. As he said, no day was too long and no work was too hard because he loved his work with his horses.

The original idea behind this book was because so many people had said that one should be written. When the pain became too much, I found that by placing a tape-recorder next to him and just letting him talk in his own way, his mind went back in time and away from the pain. He would just sit and talk and what comes through is full of social history. The poverty and hardship in the early years, today we can only imagine. He started off walking the stallion to the mares on the farms, then there was the coming of the cattle float to take the stallion around and with the coming of the cattle float was the coming of the tractor, and the heavy horse left the land. So Jack was involved with showing and the breeding of foals for other countries to work them. Artificial insemination saw an entire revolution in the basic breeding of the heavy horse. Jack's knowledge of these heavy horse breeds could not unfortunately be passed on through the tapes, but only through a life's time experience of handling, working and 'living and breathing' horses.

So to carry on the story: Simon and Crusader continued with their careers in the gymkhana world, but unfortunately all things must come to an end with horses – and their riders! But during this period there were several of Jack's grandchildren who went on to ride He enjoyed his time with them at the local gymkhanas, but time stops still for no one and they all went their various ways. Some got married and in turn produced another generation of great-grandchildren for Jack and Margaret.

Jack then came across two Suffolk geldings, Duke and Dale, which he used to take round to various shows. They became his constant companions, together with his Collie dog. There is a lovely picture on page 139 of them together. Duke and Dale were acquired when Jack was seeing to some horses owned by Paul Rackham. They were among a group of horses in a field at Scoulton, and Jack decided he would like these, and purchased them from Mr Rackham for his own.

Jack had the use of this building near 'The Laurels', at Morley St Botolph. He is pictured here, deep in thought, with Duke and Dale, his Suffolk geldings.

Sovereign, owned by Paul Rackham. Jack was 72 when Sovereign won the Supreme Championship, and was obviously delighted. He is said to have remarked: 'Having won here today, that only leaves two ambitions in my life – to live to 100, and then to be shot dead by a jealous husband!'

Suffolk horses running across to greet Jack when he went to feed them.

He still continued to go and see other people with horses, and spent many a day at various shows. He was also a great supporter and one of the founder members of the Worstead Festival. The picture below shows Jack with Paul Rackham's Easton Count at the Worstead Festival in July 2000.

Jack always took infinite pride in the presentation of his horses.

It was Jack who decided in the 1990s that he would have a yearly event – a ploughing day, which got called 'Jack's Day'. Several of the horse fraternity would get together and have friendly competitions involving ploughing with these gentle giants. This went on for several years. The winners would all get a rosette and a horse brass – and a good day was had by all! It was even reported in the ECHHA magazine, including the following poem written by John Ellis:

Rosettes and horse brasses from Jack's ploughing days.

Although November's dull and grey,
Jack Juby holds a working day.
Sometimes the weather is wet and cold,
But horsemen turn out, brave and bold.
Pairs of Shires take to the plough,
Their stalwart owners show us how.
Suffolk Punches pull plough and harrow,
While others use what they can borrow!
Jack's always up and down,
Always smiling, never a frown.
The standard of work is always high,
Makes 'old timers' heave a nostalgic sigh.
We onlookers always enjoy our day,
And thank old Jack for a pleasant display.
Now Jack's been awarded the M.B.E.,
What worthier recipient could there be?

Jack ploughing at one of 'Jack's Days', with Duke and Dale. Jack so thoroughly enjoyed his ploughing and described it nostalgically: 'You've got your pair of horses and you are in a little world of your own, just you and your horses. And following the plough, there's a certain smell comes from the land and the corn stubble, and the sound of the plough cutting – and you sense the power of the horses.'

'Jack's Day': the first ploughing match at Thickthorn Farm, 1991.

Jack at 'Jane's Day', a ploughing match at Quidenham – the last ploughing match Jack saw.

On the farm where he worked with the horses, showing and breeding continued until the death of Roger Peacock in 1998. Jack's beloved Lime Claude had by this time died, and although Jack continued to keep an eye on the horses, a natural progression of time and the final selling of the farm left him in a kind of semi-retirement. But he still had this itching in his blood for helping other people with their heavy horses – or in fact any horse if they needed him.

With the selling of Lime Tree Farm, Jack had to leave his tied cottage, and he moved to Hingham to retire, in 2001. He wasn't keen on the central heating though! But he still continued to go to all the shows and was often accompanied by his old friend Kenny Eaglen. They used to go to a lot of horse events together.

At the end of the 'Spring Working Day' in 1992. The photo was used by ECHHA. It shows (l–r) Ivan Cooke, Geoff Womack, Kenny Eaglen, Jack Juby, Dave Goodwin, Sam Stacey.

In the year 2001 there came an invitation to a Buckingham Palace garden party and Jack and his sister Edna went off and had a wonderful time. But later that year tragedy struck, and the baby of his family, Mavis, died at the very early age of 46. This hit both Jack and Margaret – a shock really that Jack was never to get over. It happened on their 64th wedding anniversary, but Jack being Jack, he had a ploughing match coming up two weeks later and his concern was not to let anybody down. A two-minutes silence was held in memory of Mavis.

In November of the same year, a letter was received from Downing Street (ironically dated 9 November, which would have been Mavis's birthday) to say he had been put forward for an M.B.E. Anybody knowing him can only imagine how difficult it was for him to keep that quiet until 1 January! How proud he was! There was a small family party held for him and the phone didn't stop ringing. Cards and messages of congratulations came in from all over the country. But unfortunately Jack became dogged with ill health and he was unable to go to Buckingham Place to receive his award. It was presented by the local postman, Mr Evan Hall. The M.B.E. was awarded to him for his 'services to heavy horses'. All those years of hard work and dedication had been noted.

Opposite: Letter from Downing Street notifying Jack of his M.B.E., ironically dated the same day as Mavie's birthday.

Jack and Edna at the Buckingham Palace Garden Party, 2001.

'Jack's Day' 2001, at which a two-minute silence was observed for Jack and Margaret's daughter 'Mavie'.

10 DOWNING STREET
LONDON SW1A 2AA

SECRETARY FOR APPOINTMENTS

W E Chapman

IN CONFIDENCE   9th November 2001

Dear Sir,

    The Prime Minister has asked me to inform you, in strict confidence, that he has it in mind, on the occasion of the forthcoming list of New Year Honours, to submit your name to The Queen with a recommendation that Her Majesty may be graciously pleased to approve that you be appointed a Member of the Order of the British Empire (MBE) .

    Before doing so, the Prime Minister would be glad to know that this would be agreeable to you. I should therefore be grateful if you would complete the enclosed form and send it to me by return of post.

    If you agree that your name should go forward and The Queen accepts the Prime Minister's recommendation, the announcement will be made in the New Year Honours List. You will receive no further communication before the List is published. Recipients will be notified of the arrangements for receiving their award within five months of the announcement.

                    I am, Sir
                    Your obedient Servant,

William Chapman

                    WILLIAM CHAPMAN

J Juby Esq
33 Greenacres
Hingham
Norfolk
NR9 4HG

Jack, proud of his medal, at the Royal Norfolk Show, 2002.

Left: *Family party to celebrate the M.B.E.*

Below: *Order that came with the M.B.E.*

Elizabeth the Second, *by the Grace of God of the United Kingdom of Great Britain and Northern Ireland and of Her other Realms and Territories Queen, Head of the Commonwealth, Defender of the Faith and Sovereign of the Most Excellent Order of the British Empire to Our trusty and well beloved* **John Juby Esquire**

Greeting

Whereas *We have thought fit to nominate and appoint you to be an Ordinary Member of the Civil Division of Our said Most Excellent Order of the British Empire*

We do *by these presents grant unto you the Dignity of an Ordinary Member of Our said Order and hereby authorise you to have hold and enjoy the said Dignity and Rank of an Ordinary Member of Our aforesaid Order together with all and singular the privileges thereunto belonging or appertaining.*

Given *at Our Court at Saint James's under Our Sign Manual and the Seal of Our said Order this Thirty-first day of December 2001 in the Fiftieth year of Our Reign.*

By the Sovereign's Command.

Grand Master.

Grant of the Dignity of an Ordinary Member of the Civil Division of the Order of the British Empire to John Juby, Esq.

Jack and Margaret celebrated their 65th wedding anniversary together – 66 years in total. Even during his ill-health, he maintained that boyish glint in his eye and his wonderful sense of humour. It was during this year that he said 'I won't see another Royal Norfolk Show.' We knew he couldn't physically walk around the show, so Janet Skidmore and our family hired a disabled buggy, for each of the two days. He was so delighted, and enjoyed every minute of it. But of course by this time he was heavily medicated, and with our determination that he should have a good quality of life, was able to enjoy what was to be his last Royal Norfolk Show.

Unfortunately Jack's health was deteriorating and the tapes had to stop, but his mind was still clear and with the aid of carers and family, he was able to remain at home until the very end, when he was moved to Priscilla Bacon, a wonderful hospice. He was very down to earth and even phoned his old friend Derek Spanton to arrange for a horse to be at his funeral and discuss what he wanted. On March 30th, 2004, Jack died.

Jack and Margaret at the MBE celebration.

The funeral was a celebration of his life so everything had to be planned down to the last detail. He had told me that he wanted 'Lord of the Dance' when he went into the church. I decided that 'The day thou gavest Lord, has ended,' should also be included, because I remember him singing that when he went into the hospice and 'Morning Has Broken', to see him into the new world. His old friend Ray Hubbard played on his melodeon and Maggie Secker of Radio Norfolk recited a poem. Philip Ryder-Davies gave a lovely tribute about Jack's life. As he left the church we played Gracie Fields 'Wish me luck as I go on my way'. Finally Ray played 'Joe the Carrier Lad' on his melodeon. In fact, Jack was clapped from the churchyard as if he was leaving the show ring (he was always clapped out of the ring). It was a true celebration of his life and even today people remember that day with affection, as they had always remembered Jack with affection.

Jack on his invalid scooter at his last Royal Norfolk Show, 2003.

The following year we contacted the Royal Norfolk Show and it was decided that a trophy should be given in his memory. There is now at the Royal Norfolk Show a 'Jack Juby M.B.E. Perpetual Challenge Trophy', for the best Percheron or Suffolk Stallion. I knew that he would have wanted this class, because above all he remained a Stallion Man.

Jack's funeral 13 April, 2004, 'the last ride of a horseman'. Jack's funeral cart pulled by Shire horse Nayland Grey King (Jim), leaves Morley St Botolph's Church after the service. A single red rose was placed on his coffin and on an afternoon of brilliant sunshine, hundreds gathered from all parts of the country to show their respects.

Outside Morley St Botolph Church before Jack's funeral service. On the left is Jack's long-term friend Kenny Eaglen. Next to him is another friend Derek Spanton with Jack's daughter Alison, and his Collie, Tay.

Jack Juby Perpetual Challenge Trophy, presented at the Royal Norfolk Show in 2005.

Cup being presented at the Royal Norfolk Show by Alison in June 2005. The judge was Nigel Oakley and the trophy was won by Fiona Fleming's Colony Millennium.

Margaret looks proudly on with her two daughters Rosemarie, left, and Alison, right, at the Royal Norfolk Show in 2005.

APPENDIX ONE
TRIBUTES TO JACK

*W*hen Jack Juby died on 30 March 2004, it is not surprising that a number of tributes to him were written and obituaries appeared, reflecting the high regard in which he was held among the heavy horse fraternity.

David Banham *now living in Lincolnshire, recalls many a day spent working with Jack and his Shires, and he contributes the following memories of Jack:*

'When I lived at Suton, (near Wymondham), it was about the 1990s, I had a phone call from Jack:

'Are you busy today?
I replied, 'No, Why?'
'I have got a stallion down at the marsh (Acle) and I want to get him home, can I use your lorry?'
'Yes,' was the reply, and later that morning we went off to the marsh. On the way I asked him how old it was. He told me about five. We had long conversations about its parents, and how it would never be a Lime Claude.

Below: *Jack with two of David Banham's Shires.*

Dick Jeeves Collection

We arrived at Acle and his words to me were, 'Stay where you are, boy, I will go and catch him.' I just said, 'When was the last time he was caught?' He had one of his wonderful rope halters in his hand and he said, 'A bloody long time ago, two or three years I suppose – never had to touch his old feet.' He walked out to the horse, saying 'whoa me lad, whoa me lad', in Jack's way – no rush. He patted him two or three times on the neck. I was thinking, 'You are close enough – *catch him.*' But slowly and surely he slid the rope over his neck and the halter over his ears and nose, and with a little jerk to let the horse know he was there, walked towards the lorry.

Then the fun began at the bottom of the ramp. The horse stood on its hind legs, thrashing its front ones in the air. This happened several times.
Jack said, 'I will tie him to the gate post to let him have a little pull.' This did not work very well, and he nearly had the gate post out of the ground. Jack said, 'Well, we won't give up. You have got a draw-bar on your lorry?' I thought, 'Whatever are we going to do now?'
He said, 'There is a corral about three quarters of a mile up the roadway. If I just put the rope on the end of your draw-bar, I will hold the other end. You drive off and I will walk with him.' I set off and every ten to twelve yards going forward, I could feel the horse pulling against the lorry, and in the mirror I could see Jack's hand waving me slowly forward. We arrived at the corral and after a lot of patting his neck and talking to the horse, Jack finally got him onto the lorry.

On the journey home I asked Jack if he had ever had one he couldn't load. He said, 'No, but that old bugger was the closest.' He said, 'I did have one I couldn't *un*load.' I said, 'What did you do?'
He said, 'You know that church down at the marsh, what I did was get some long rope and tied it to the church gate, tipped the lorry a little bit and slowly moved forward. It came off as good as gold. What a horseman! And a very dear friend.

Trevor Weston *adds the following:*

Jack was the one and only true horseman and friend I was very proud to have known. He had very special ways which I don't think I will ever come across again in my lifetime dealing with horses.

Jack, I can remember it to this day threw my daughter Jemma up on the back of a heavy horse when she was, I think, two years old and to this day she has still got the Juby horse bug. He was so encouraging to young people wanting to make a start with horses. He just wanted them to have as much out of horses as he had had. I can remember him saying to Jemma, 'If you want a horse you must look after it seven days a week and you don't miss a day, young lady. If you look after him, he will reward you in kindness. He is a very intelligent and noble animal, and don't you ever forget that – and she has not.

As time went on, my daughter Jemma was given a very small pony called Kipper to ride at Crows Hall. She used to go out with me on a leading rein, until she was able to ride on her own and I also used to jump over small jumps running alongside her. Very often dear old Jack would turn up out of the blue and he would take time to chat to Jemma and take her to one side and ask how she was getting on. Imagine how she felt when she got off that pony. She would be beaming! Jack was so inspiring to young people and I am sure a lot of people the same age as my Jemma are very grateful for his little chats.

I have also seen him load horses where other people could not, and I have seen people stand with their mouths open so wide you could drive a horsebox in!

I can also remember Jack was a great fan of binder twine. If something broke, he always said,' You can't beat a bit of twine to get you out of a muddle, boy!' – and it was evident everywhere.

I can remember hearing a tale that Jack had found one of Roger Peacock's heavies caught up on an old fence stake and Jack had called the vet. When the vet saw the horse he said, 'I will go back to the car for a sedative.' And by the time the vet had got back to Jack and the horse, Jack – as small as he was – had got the horse on the floor ready for the vet, much to his amazement. I just can't imagine how he done it. I would have liked to have seen him do it.

On one occasion at a show, Jack walked past me and said, 'You haven't seen me walk past you if anyone asks.' He winked at me and I knew instantly he was up to no good. He had got that mischievous look in his eye as he slipped off out of the yard and out of sight. I believe he slipped into a stable in the yard and hid up.

Lo and behold, after 15 minutes, this little man dressed like a tramp came out. He had got a dirty old coat on with a stick on his shoulder with a little canvas bag attached to it, a grey horse tail for a wig and a small hat. There was string round his middle, with his shirt hanging out – and he stunk! He must have rubbed some muck on himself to get the effect. He came shuffling into the field, and I instantly knew who it was as he looked up at me and winked, and carried on walking. He went round the horseboxes begging for food and water and was told, 'go away you dirty old man!' And a lot of people were quite put out with this dirty little man on the scrounge. I think I am right in saying they complained to Mr Rose. They did not know who he was – it was so funny. That memory of Jack will be with me for the rest of my life.

I remember clearly at Jack's funeral, the horse pulling the cart, and as things went very quiet, the horse neighed at just the right moment, so much as to say, 'Good old Jack'. And I can still hear the melodeon the gentleman played as I stood in the churchyard with many others. It was so moving and memorable. Yes I had tears running down my cheeks. I have lost family and work-mates but believe you me, I knew I had lost a genuine old Norfolk friend.

The Garner family *of Hales Stud, Willingham,*
added their memories:

My first memories are when I was about 13 years old and the first job of the morning after sleeping on a straw bed at the shows was to make the first pot of tea. Father used to say, 'Give Jack a call' as he would be busy in the horse lines feeding round. We would share the first cup of tea and discuss the day's proceedings.

Jack was always a mine of information and I would glean as much knowledge as possible from him. We only spent a few days of the year together so it was very important to me this time with him.

One sunny day at the East of England show, Hannah, our youngest daughter, bought a toy pony and Jack patiently made a halter for it. She was thrilled to bits with it. Jack used to visit our farm at Willingham to see what young Percheron stock was available. We also used to keep a few ponies and on one occasion Jack purchased one of his best jumping ponies called Simon.

As the years progressed Jack always had time for the younger members of all heavy horse families. It always amazed us, and everyone in the showing community, how Jack was able to take his Suffolk gelding and wagon to all major county shows. He managed to do all this so well and at such a great age. He never gave up.

Jack will always be fondly remembered as a true horseman.

'Jack Juby, Suffolk Horses and a Personal View',
by Philip Ryder-Davies.
As a practising vet, and friend, **Philip Ryder-Davies**
contributes a special perspective on Jack.

In an extremely varied life I have met a large number of people, but of these a few, because of their character, stand out as personalities whom I will not only never forget but will remember in detail. One of these is Jack Juby. He, like many heavy horse showmen, was a small man, with an engaging smile and was wonderful company. Horses were his whole life and he had a mine of knowledge which he was ready to impart to anyone who was interested in horses and was prepared to listen; they could learn so much from him. He had a great memory and could relate so many anecdotes about horses and people from the past, and I never saw him without being told a joke, usually one that could be repeated in mixed company.

I first met him on our honeymoon, which consisted of three days in Norfolk in deep snow. We went to see the Gurney family's herd of British White Cattle, looked at rare poultry and visited Roger Peacock's stud of Percheron Horses with Jack in attendance. Our next meeting was at the Centenary Woodbridge Show, the breed Show for Suffolk Horses. At that time, I was a student in Newmarket and had been given the day off to attend this special Show. Roger Clark, already making a considerable name for himself with Suffolks, needed someone to lead one of his horses in the Grand Parade and Jack said, seeing me standing there, 'He'll do it,' which I did.

As the years went by, I saw more and more of him at shows and appreciated his friendship and the knowledge he was always prepared to share. My greatest contact with him was cemented when Roger Peacock asked me to go and castrate some colts for him, as I did this job with the horses standing. I arrived at the farm in Morley, got out of the car, walked across the yard to see three huge heads over the box doors, eyes like saucers and nostrils like the entrance to Blackwall Tunnel with steam coming out of each. Even though I did not know at the time that the colts, two year olds, had not been handled from being weaned to being brought into the yard on the previous day, I still looked at the job with considerable trepidation. As there was no one about, I decided my best plan was to disappear and telephone from somewhere to say that I had been unable to get to Morley for some reason. At that point, however, Jack arrived so my escape was foiled. I had not, of course, appreciated his consummate horsemanship because none of them moved and it should be added at that time, we did not have the powerful sedatives that we have today. One of the colts did pick one hind foot off the ground by about five inches and Jack apologized profusely.

We subsequently castrated a considerable number of colts together. While so well known as a heavy horseman, Jack bred and owned some very good showjumping ponies and he had acquired a thoroughbred mare who was extremely dangerous. If Jack could not handle a horse then matters were serious. We castrated three of her sons and as they had inherited their mother's disposition, I can assure you that I would have had difficulty doing the job unless Jack had been holding them and probably would not have offered to do it. I remember him saying about the first one, 'This will not be too easy,' and I recall thinking that if Jack said that then it was probably time to take the matter seriously. I had complete faith in him and remembered one day I examined sixteen mares, doing rectal examinations to see if they were in foal; none of them had been handled very much, but I was quite happy with him at the head.

Jack could do any job with horses. He had been a stallion leader when stallions were travelled, had broken in horses for work, shown them in-hand and had driven four horse teams in the show ring. While we all think of him as a Percheron man, he had worked with Shires and he did have a soft spot for Suffolks. Before going to work for Geoffrey Peacock he had worked for Geo. C & T.C. Knights of Melton Constable whose Stody Stud was one of the biggest in the 1950's. He had led the Suffolk Stallion Sandringham Scapa 7084, bred by King George VI and then the property of A.A. Walker, of Watering Farm, East Dereham.

Jack showed Suffolks for Paul Rackham of Bridgham, both in-hand and in turn-out classes using the wonderfully restored vehicles which Paul Rackham has collected. He continued to show for Paul Rackham until a very ripe old age, although he looked much younger than he was. At the Royal Show in later years, he had, as his groom, Pat Flood, a leading Shire turn-out man. The combined age of the two was considerable. I was braiding my own gelding's tail at the Royal when the two of them came and watched my performance at the job, which has never been achieved to a very high standard. I told Jack that if he stood and watched he would pick up some useful tips.' Yes,' he said, 'Everything I know I got from watching you,' and Pat said 'And everything I know I got from watching him.'

That great Suffolk Horse exhibitor Charlie Saunders continued to keep a few horses after his right hand woman and mainstay Jennie Cauldwell had died, and he relied on Jack for help with them. Despite the sometimes inconvenient telephone calls, Jack would always go and assist Charlie when asked to do so; his nature was such that he could not have refused to go to the aid of another horseman.

He acquired two Suffolk geldings Duke and Dale from Paul Rackham and soon he had these broken in for work so that he could go to ploughing matches with them. When the Suffolk Show started Suffolk Punch shoeing competitions, and I had the task of finding the horses for these, one of the people I could count on for help was Jack. He was not only ready to bring his horses, and others, but I knew the horses would behave properly and have good feet.

My own approach to showing horses is to panic, and to have serious anxiety over getting horses ready to go into the ring on time. My abiding memory of Jack, on the other hand, is to see him on his own, tying a horse up outside a box and then doing the mane and tail up with a horse that never moved. This would be done with no sign of speed and everything would be ready on time.

He and his wife Margaret would sit on deck chairs by their lorry, with a sheep dog and would both be a delight, with Margaret's laugh part of the pleasure. She found so much humour in what Jack did; this must have been part of the success of their long marriage. She and their children looked out of the window one afternoon to see Jack coming up the garden path dressed in her nightdress with his trousers rolled up to reveal big boots with a chamber pot on his head.

His extraordinary memory could fail him occasionally; he had taken six Percherons to the Norfolk Show and his daughter Alison, then aged 13, had gone to help him. All the horses had done very well so a reporter for the Eastern Daily Press had gone to interview him and had been given details of their breeding and precise ages. The reporter was taken with this very young girl assisting him so asked Jack how old she was. 'I'm not sure,' he said and to Alison he called, 'How old are you gal?'

It was a privilege to have known Jack and a great honour to have been asked to give the address at his funeral and especially to be part of an over-flowing congregation of people who had held him in such high regard and with such affection.

This obituary appeared in the 'Heavy Horse World', Summer 2004.

We were all deeply saddened to learn of the death of Jack Juby on 30 March, for it marks the passing of one of the truly accomplished horsemen of his generation and a stalwart supporter of the Percheron breed in this country. He was a man of courage who maintained a steadfast belief in the value and utility of the heavy horse for certain work, even during the times when the very existence of the species was most threatened.

Jack worked for and served three generations of the Peacock family on their farms near Morley in Norfolk, working tirelessly to promote the interests of the heavy horse generally and the Peacock family's outstanding 'Lime' prefix in particular. The late Roger Peacock, a former president of this society, had forged cordial links with the powerful French horse society and was instrumental in bringing to this country horses of important French blood lines. Jack was his able and enthusiastic right-hand man, a most competent and wise horseman who nurtured and trained the stock in his care to the very highest level. His style was not to hector or dominate, rather he sought to encourage and widen a handler's perception of the horse's capabilities, quietly and with good humour, for Jack understood horses perhaps to an infinite degree – which few can claim.

He was a staunch supporter of the British Percheron Horse Society and served on its council for a time. He was prominent with the Peacock horses at all major shows, gaining many premier prizes and awards for the outstanding manner in which the Lime prefix stock was put forward. How often we can recall the sight of the slight figure of Jack Juby, in his traditional grey smock coat, somewhat bandy legs, pounding along, with a huge Percheron stallion in hand, before an impassive-looking judge at a major show. Both horse and handler were in perfect harmony.

We can also recall the excellent gatherings at the summer shows held at Carl Boyde's farm in Surrey when Jack would parade his beloved Lime Claude stallion, smart and fresh after the long journey from Norfolk, to 'show the folks what a real Percheron looks like!' – this said with a twinkling eye and a meaningful grin for good measure.

It was with Claude that Jack scored a further triumph, for the horse was used as a model by Joel, internationally acclaimed sculptor, for the statuettes he created for leading art galleries throughout Europe. The work had demanded very many hours of posing by the horse – which Jack ensured to perfection.

A sculpture of Lime Claude's head by Joel. It was presented to Roderick Watts, 8 May 1993, by the Percheron Horse Society, in appreciation. Lime Claude was Jack's beloved stallion.

To us, Jack was of course indelibly associated with the heavy horse, and the Percheron especially, yet he was as well known, even a by-word, in respect of light horses. Throughout East Anglia he was acknowledged as an authority on horses – all sorts of horses – his experience and kindness ever available to the youngest novices with their little ponies. So many people of all ages and from all sections of the equine world have benefited from his wisdom and skill – he will be sorely missed.

Jack was awarded the M.B.E. in 2002 for 'services to heavy horses'. It was a fitting recognition, as were the countless other awards he received from leading agricultural and equine bodies, for his was a long and full life.

We in the Percheron Horse Society mourn Jack's passing as yet another irreplaceable loss from an age-group who kept the interest in heavy horses alive in extremely difficult times – Jim Young, Edward Sneath, Stanley Garner, Roger Peacock, Tom Sampson, all stalwarts devoted to the Percheron. Our world is an infinitely sadder place without them.

In the April/May 2004 edition of the British Percheron Horse Society Newsletter, **Linda V. Chapman,** *Council member and former Treasuer of the Society, wrote this obituary:*

Many people pass in and out of our lives as we go about our daily business. Occasionally, there are characters that have a profound and lasting effect on us. Jack Juby was one such character that had just that effect on me. He welcomed me to the heavy horse world and always made time to give me advice, and impart some of the vast knowledge that he had of the draught horses he loved. I felt privileged to receive that knowledge from such an eminent horseman and hearing such funny tales of the past was a joy.

I will never forget the times spent in his company especially one in particular that still wakes a smile. I was visiting Jack and his wife Margaret at Morley, and the time came to feed the various horses he had dotted about the Norfolk countryside. Into the horsebox we climbed, the letters JJ's GG's emblazoned on the side; and proceeded to hurtle (no exaggeration) around the narrow back roads of Norfolk delivering mangolds to

horses of all shapes, sizes and colours. And all the while the stories flowed – just one memory of many.

A giant of a man involved with the giants of the horse world. He will be sadly missed.

In the ECHHA Newsletter, May 2004, **Judy Christopher** *wrote this obituary:*

Jack Juby M.B.E. died in the early hours of Tuesday 30th March 2002 after a long illness. He was 84 years old. He leaves a widow, Margaret, two sons, two daughters (a third daughter died recently), twelve grandchildren plus great-grandchildren and great-great-grandchildren.

One of seven children of a road mender, Jack never liked school and was always glad of an excuse to exchange the classroom for the farmyard.

He had a lifelong love of horses and helped to break his first horse at the age of ten and, in 1937, went to work for the Peacock family at Morley St Botolph. He spent almost sixty years working for four generations of the Peacock family, including showing their Percheron horses.

He also worked for some of the top breeders in the country including for a few months, Ivan Cooke, a former chairman of the Suffolk Horse Society, who said, 'I showed alongside him for more that fifty years. He would help anyone and had a tremendous knowledge of horses.'

He didn't miss a Royal Norfolk Show in sixty years, and, at some time or other, had met most of the Royal Family.

For most of his life, the family lived at Morley St Botolph, but Jack and Margaret moved a short distance to Hingham about four years ago Jack's funeral took place on Tuesday 13 April 2002 at Morley St Botolph church, in glorious sunshine.

Inside, the church was packed, with standing room only, and the service was relayed to 100 or so mourners standing outside, all wanting to celebrate Jack's life.

For his final journey, Jack was brought to, and taken, from the church by a Shire horse, Nayland Grey King (Jim), driven by Derek Spanton and escorted by Kenny

Eaglen. The service was conducted by the Reverend Shirley Holt and, as the coffin entered the church, Ray Hubbard played a tune on his melodeon .

Maggie Secker of Radio Norfolk recited a poem written especially for the occasion and then Philip Ryder-Davies, one of his oldest friends, gave the address.

He had met Jack thirty eight years ago whilst visiting Norfolk, from neighbouring Suffolk, on his honeymoon.

Jack was made an M.B.E. in 2002 for his services to the heavy horse world, much to the delight of his family, his friends, indeed everyone who knew him.

Philip Ryder-Davies said his abiding memory of Jack was leaving the Royal Show in 2000. As he drove down the busy M6, in the inside lane, he spotted a familiar yellow horse-box in his wing mirror. It was Jack at the wheel, in the middle lane, tearing down the motorway, with a slightly white-faced friend in the passenger seat. A few days later, he asked the friend why she looked so pale 'You would, if you knew that Jack was playing a mouth organ at the same time!'

Jack, you would have enjoyed the day, and thank you, for all the memories.

Above and below: *At the Royal Norfolk Show 2002, being interviewed about his M.B.E.* Dick Jeeves Collection

At the Royal Norfolk Show 2002, being interviewed about his M.B.E.   Dick Jeeves Collection

APPENDIX TWO
HORSE CURES

*T*he well-used notebook that was Jack's secret book of horse cures was typically owned by horsemen everywhere, and was generally reckoned to be the passport to a job. It contained most probably the accumulated wisdom of generations, passed down from horseman to horseman. For interest we include a few of these cures, with the suggestion that they are not tried out – just in case!

1 To make a horse do well, eat well and get him into fair condition

  1 oz.   Black Hellebore
  1 oz.   Gentian
  1 oz.   Pitre
  1 oz.   Paradise
  1 oz.   White Hellebore
  1 oz.   Cumin
  1 oz.   Fenugreek

Give one tablespoonful every other night in his feed, after water

2 For the mange

  ½ lb.   Black Brimstone
  ¼ pt.   Turpentine
  ½ pt.   Train oil

Mix together and rub the mixture well over the affected parts.

3 For Foot Rot or Epidemia

  ½ oz.   Oil of Vitrol
  ½ oz.   Verdigris
  ½ oz.   Honey
  ¼ oz.   Sugar of lead
  ¼ oz.   Red Precipitate
  ¼ oz.   Goulard

Mix well together and pare the feet well before applying the dressing.

4 Brittle Hoofs

Dress twice weekly with the following ointment.

  1 lb.   Oil of Tar
  1 lb.   Yellow Ware

12 oz. Glycerine
6 lb.   Lard

During hot weather it will greatly help by standing in water or clay puddles.

5 For Colic or Gripes in Horses or for blown beasts
1 oz. Sweet Pitre
1 oz. Oil of Peppermint
1 oz. Sweet oil
1 oz. Laudanum

To be given in one drink in a pint of warm beer and it will ease in 20 minutes.

6 How to manage a Vicious Horse so as to do anything with him
Take Oil of Fennell, oil of Cinnamon, oil of Thyme, oil of Rosemary, Tincture of opium, Tincture Arnica, illontara, oil of Nutmeg, oil of Anniseed, one ounce of Lunas Powder.

Take a little of the powder and put a few drops out of each bottle on it so as to make a paste and the air must be kept from it after you have made it. Rub a little on your whip and on your hands and stroke them over the horse's nostrils a few times. This must be all kept in separate bottles.

7 To keep Flies off Cattle
1 oz. Oil of aspro
1 oz. Oil of Elder
1 oz. Oil of Tar
1 oz. Dregs of Hartshorn
1 oz. Sulphur
1 oz. Assafoctida

Mix well and apply.

8 To Manage a Entire Horse
10 drops Oil of Origanum
15 drops Oil of Anniseed
15 drops Oil of Nutmegs
15 drops Oil of Cumins
15 drops Oil of Fennel
15 drops Oil of Penny Royal

Drop the above oils on a quarter of ounce of Lumis or Orris powder into and apply it to the ear, nostril or tongue.

Example pages from Jack's secret book of horse cures.

So when my day on earth is done,

What though my memory fade;

I know I'll sleep quite peacefully

When in Norfolk I am laid.

Jack's headstone with a carving of a hay cart being pulled by a heavy horse, and with a Border Collie walking beside.